Fin de Siècle PRINTS POSTERS & PROSE

The Collection Of Erwin Raible & Robert Hoskins

Introduction by Patricia Eckert Boyer
Text by Erwin Raible

Taft Museum
Cincinnati

A catalogue published on the occasion
of the exhibition in Cincinnati,
September 14 through October 21, 1990

On the cover:
Pierre Bonnard, proof for cover of **La lithographie originale en couleurs,** 1898, lithograph printed in dark gray, h. 21.5 x w. 18.5 cm.

Design: Erwin Raible with Frank Satogata, Satogata/Vollmer Inc., Cincinnati
Printing: Royal Offset, New York
Typesetting: Harlan Typographic, Cincinnati

Library of Congress Catalog Card Number: 90-62623
ISBN: 0-915577-21-6

PRINTED IN THE UNITED STATES OF AMERICA

The Taft Museum is the first Fine Arts Fund institution and gratefully acknowledges its continuing support as well as that of the City of Cincinnati, County of Hamilton, and Ohio Arts Council. The Museum also receives frequent grants from the National Endowment for the Arts and Institute of Museum Services, both federal agencies.

FINE ARTS FUND
ENRICH YOUR LIFE.

Accredited by the American Association of Museums

Funded Through
Ohio Arts Council
727 East Main Street
Columbus, Ohio 43205-1796
(614) 466-2613

CITY OF CINCINNATI
OHIO

To Rob

Foreword

Fin de Siècle Prints, Posters & Prose: The Collection of Erwin Raible and Robert Hoskins cannot be presented without acknowledging how the collection originated and why we are honored to premier it at the Taft Museum. Working with collectors is the most satisfying aspect of museum work: helping collectors to realize the dimensions of their achievement through exhibitions is even more rewarding.

The collection Erwin Raible is building serves as a memorial to his companion in life, Robert Hoskins, who died in 1984. Hoskins grew up in Glendale, Ohio, and graduated from Cincinnati Country Day School. He also graduated from Yale University and taught in eastern schools before returning to Cincinnati. Here, he received a Master's degree from the University of Cincinnati and then taught at Indian Hill High School.

Erwin Raible was from Western Hills and went to the district's high school before enrolling at the University of Cincinnati's College of Design, Architecture, Art and Planning to study art and art education. After graduation in 1967 he taught at Whittier School before joining with other arts teachers to found the Cincinnati School for Creative and Performing Arts in 1973-74. Hoskins joined that faculty the following year.

Living together during these years Hoskins and Raible began to collect Chinese porcelains, and their research for those purchases led them to the Taft Museum where they were advised by Director Katherine Hanna and her assistant, Jan Weigel. When the museum celebrated the 50th anniversary of its charter in 1977, the two men lent porcelains from their collection to be used as containers for flowers throughout the house.

During the summer of 1978 Hoskins and Raible decided to move to New York and to become owners and managers of nightclubs. Hoskins had once owned a bar near the university campus in Cincinnati and enjoyed the conviviality of the barkeeper's job. Raible's interest in the performing arts guided their planning toward the cabaret, and during the next six years they would run three different establishments. Posters purchased to decorate a club form the nucleus of the collection we are presenting.

Since Hoskins's death, Raible has concentrated his collecting activities in the field of turn-of-the-century French graphic arts, enlarging on and refining the couple's previous selections. A long-standing interest in the career of Toulouse-Lautrec and the print techniques he used led Raible to his equally famous colleagues Bonnard and Vuillard and to less well known artists such as Ibels and Steinlen. In his own acknowledgments Raible mentions all those who have encouraged his dedication and guided him toward scholarly methods of study and acquisition. With all their help, the collection still remains a highly personal assembly reflecting Raible's artistic tastes and memories of his dearest companion.

Three years ago Erv Raible offered the Taft Museum the opportunity to exhibit the collection once it had reached an advanced stage of development. That time has come, and I am very proud to show it and to publish it. Robert Hoskins was my friend too.

Ruth K. Meyer
Director, Taft Museum

Acknowledgments

A collection does not come about by accident. There are a number of widely varying collections among the things with which I live. Robert Hoskins and I collected together; I am still a collector, always was, and always will be. There is always a specific reason behind why a group of objects is collected; there is always that treasured "first object" from which the collection begins.

The following acknowledgments are for the print collection contained within this exhibition. Almost all collectors at some point want to blame someone else for their often all-consuming obsession and acknowledge those who knowingly or unknowingly helped in the evolution of the collection with their advice, their knowledge, their sources, their encouragement, their guidance, and their friendship and love.

So at the risk of sounding like a cross between "thank you's" at the *Academy Awards* and an episode of *This Is Your Life*—the acknowledgments:

To my parents, Erwin and Dorothy Raible, my grandmother Jenny Weiss, and my adopted grandparents Harry and Anna V. Thomas for encouraging my personal art and my interest in the art of others and collecting. To Robert Hoskins, the love of my life, for 17 years of happiness and love, for my strength, my courage, and the ability to survive. To Marilyn Goodfellow, my seventh-grade art teacher who was primarily responsible for my becoming an art teacher and who presented me with a Toulouse-Lautrec poster book to study, forever planting the seeds of interest in Lautrec, Paris, and cabaret. To Patricia Eckert Boyer for asking if I would be interested in lending pieces to "The Nabis and the Parisian Avant-Garde" exhibition at Rutgers University/Zimmerli Museum and reopening the door to the art world that I had left 10 years earlier as well as for her friendship, knowledge, and talent. To Herbert Schimmel for the landmark Toulouse-Lautrec exhibition at the Museum of Modern Art, New York, and for his encouraging response to my thank-you letter and inquiry about Toulouse-Lautrec and print collecting. To Anne and Arsène Bonafous-Murat, Mireille Romand and Isabelle Maurel of Paris, and Gail Chisholm and Eric Carlson of New York for their acceptance, generosity, dedication to their business, and the services they and their businesses provide for collectors and for including me as "one of the family." To Virginia and Ira Jackson for their friendship, gracious acceptance, and encouragement to me as a novice collector.

To Charles A. Haas for his expertise, patience, and many hours spent photographing the collection.

To pianist *extraordinaire* Dick Gallagher and technical director Matt Berman of Eighty-Eights piano bar and cabaret, New York, for producing the period music tapes from the illustrated sheet music accompanying this exhibition.

For their encouragement along the way: M. and Mme. Guy Apfelbaum, Nicolas Bailly, Demetre Belgis, François Boutet de Monvel, Phillip Dennis Cate, Robert Chisholm, Dominique de Latre, Ronald de Leeuw, Gertrude W. Dennis, Elizabeth Easton, Laura Gold, James Goodfriend, Conrad Graeber, Bernard LeCompte, Roberta Lehrman, Stephen Long, Jacqueline Martinet, R.G. Michel, Karen Miller, Bertha Montague, Marcel Moulin, Harriet Nyberg, M. and Mme. Hubert Prouté, Dorothy Schneiderman, Rochelle Seldin, Susan Teller, and Phillip Williams.

To my dear friend Ruth K. Meyer, Director of the Taft Museum, and her wonderfully competent staff, in particular, Assistant Director/Registrar David T. Johnson, Publications/Press Officer Cate O'Hara, Chief of Protection Services John Ring, and Museum Technician Mark Allen.

And last but by no means least, special thanks to Jack Eaton, Cynthia Crane, and my canine sidekick, Maggie, for always being there.

Erwin Raible

Introduction

The period spanning the late 1880s to c. 1900 in France was complex and troubled politically, socially, and economically; yet, at the same time, it was one of the most intense and innovative artistic periods in the history of modern art. Crucial to this accelerated development in the arts were the rise of new avenues of patronage and the expansion of opportunities in art exhibition and publication. The loss of prominence of traditional sources of patronage, coupled with the increased power and wealth of a growing bourgeoisie, had dramatically shifted the consumer market for art. While this restructuring of patronage brought artistic advancement to a halt in some circles, in others it promoted a stylistic and intellectual inventiveness of almost unparalleled intensity. At the same time, critics recognized that France was no longer a leader in the creation of industrial, or applied, art, and they called increasingly for artists to devote themselves to that arena. Partially in response to this vacuum, some artists therefore began to explore the potential of uniting the bold new language of their art with objects of a functional nature.

The graphic arts offered one means by which artists could address these issues. Prints provided multiples of an image and facilitated the application of original art to objects intended for everyday use. Creating art for a broader public would (it was hoped) elevate the general level of taste and, in turn, create a broader basis of patronage. The graphic arts were fully embraced—seemingly without bias—by many artists of the period, who explored such diverse aspects of the medium as original color lithography, on the one hand, and the photomechanical reproduction of drawings in the popular press, on the other. The Erwin Raible and Robert Hoskins collection of graphic arts includes works by Toulouse-Lautrec, Henri-Gabriel Ibels, Pierre Bonnard, Edouard Vuillard, and several of their contemporaries. These bold young artists were involved in nearly every facet of the avant-garde of the 1890s, and the works in the collection provide an insightful glimpse of this era that changed the face of modern art.

The rise of photomechanical printing techniques in the 1880s and 1890s brought about a tremendous surge in the publication of illustrated journals. Such magazines offered an alternative "exhibition space" for artists seeking exposure for their art. Among these, Toulouse-Lautrec published drawings in the press early in his career and continued to contribute illustrations through the mid-1890s. The images he designed for the press parallel his work in other media. Lautrec's first "print," *Gin Cocktail*, a photomechanical reproduction of a drawing, was published in the journal *Le courrier français* on September 26, 1886 (fig. 73). Jules Roques, the publisher of this journal devoted to the pleasures of Montmartre, regularly included photomechanical reproductions of drawings by such artists as Adolphe Willette, Jean-Louis Forain, and Hermann-Paul. Roques was a notoriously clever entrepreneur who underpaid his artists, and Lautrec was among those who experienced financial conflict with him. Lautrec allowed him to reproduce the drawing *Gin Cocktail* solely for artistic exposure, without monetary recompense, and Roques reproduced more of Lautrec's drawings in 1889. In 1891, however, when Roques sold at auction some other unpublished drawings that Lautrec had given him, Lautrec sued.[1] The dispute was apparently resolved, however, because by 1892 Roques began to reproduce his posters and prints.

During 1886-87 Lautrec's drawings were also reproduced in *Le Mirliton*, a journal published by the cabaret of the same name and owned by the infamous performer Aristide Bruant. The images appeared as stencil-colored photorelief cover illustrations, which Lautrec signed with the pseudonym "Tréclau," a transposition of the letters in his name (figs. 51, 52). In publishing a journal, Bruant followed the example set by Rodolphe Salis, owner of the Chat Noir café, whose journal, *Le chat noir*, had been illustrated and written by its habitués since 1882. Bruant had performed for the Chat Noir, and in 1885 when Salis moved to larger headquarters, Bruant converted the former Chat Noir into Le Mirliton.[2] Lautrec was a frequent visitor to both cabarets, and the black silhouettes in the background of his *Le Mirliton* cover illustration *Le dernier salut* reflect the contemporary and very popular shadow-theater plays at the Chat Noir (fig. 52).[3] During the next few years Lautrec would incorporate black and color silhouettes into many of his prints as a powerful decorative motif.[4]

Paris illustré was another early patron for Lautrec. He made four drawings that were reproduced photomechanically as illustrations for Émile Michelet's article, "L'Été á Paris," in the July 7, 1888, issue (figs. 74-75A). As Dennis Cate has noted, in three of these, Lautrec adopted a technique that was atypical for him: he used the *manière noire* method of blackening the entire surface and then scraping pigment away to reveal light areas and lines. He adopted this approach in response to the need to create an image of high contrast (black and white) to be reproduced by a photorelief process.[5]

By 1893 Lautrec's bold artistic genius was well recognized within avant-garde circles, and his contributions to the press continued: he created color images to be reproduced photomechanically as illustrations for Gustave Geffroy's "Le plaisir à Paris: Les restaurants et les cafés-concerts des Champs-Elysées," in *Figaro illustré*. In these vignettes we immediately recognize the individuals from Lautrec's world who appear in many of his original lithographs and paintings: Libert, Yvette Guilbert, and Caudieux, for example (fig. 99C), all of whom can be seen in other works in the exhibition (figs. 68, 78, 65). Lautrec illustrated articles in two subsequent issues of *Figaro illustré*: in 1894, Geffroy's sequel, "Le plaisir à Paris: Les bals et le carnaval" (no. 100, fig. 100B); and in an issue for 1895, collaborating with Romain Coolus, "La belle et la bête" (no. 101). For the inaugural issue of *Le Rire*, on November 10, 1894, Lautrec contributed a drawing titled "Yvette Guilbert in Linger, Longer, Loo!" (fig. 78). Subsequent issues of this satirical journal often included reproductions of his humorous drawings of entertainers and places of entertainment. The publishers of *Le Rire*, Félix Juven and Arsène Alexandre, also included color photomechanical reproductions of the drawings of many of Lautrec's contemporaries including Félix Vallotton, Théophile-Alexandre Steinlen, Lucien Métivet (fig. 76; no. 77), and Hermann-Paul.

By the mid-1890s color lithography had emerged as the primary original print medium, and Lautrec was one of many artists energetically exploring its decorative and expressive potential. In 1898 André Mellerio, an advocate of the medium, reviewed its recent history in *La lithographie originale en couleurs:*

> There is no one who has not made [color lithographs], who is not making them, or who will not make them. Even artists who have reached an advanced age with a glorious career behind them are interested. As for the younger artists, color prints are for them a veritable weapon which they use extensively and well. Some threw themselves into printmaking early in their careers, and found a process suited to their incipient style, and their earliest attempts showed understanding. From day to day they improve and perfect the technique, each one in an aspect fitted to his temperament—and the group continually becomes stronger.[6]

This great activity in color lithography was the result of several factors, among them the work of the commercial artist Jules Chéret whose much admired placards had graced the streets of Paris since the 1870s. Images such as that on his poster advertising *La Diaphane Poudre de Riz* (endorsed by Sarah Bernhardt) exemplify the lively formula that held universal appeal (fig. 48). In fact, in his review of the industrial arts at the Paris Universal Exposition for 1889, the art critic Roger-Marx praised Chéret as the only true *décorateur* in Paris at the time.[7] Young artists interested in the practical application of their art considered Chéret to be their mentor.

Another factor contributing to the resurgence of interest in the original print was the admiration for Japanese color woodblock prints, which had been widely available in Paris since mid-century. The stylistic quality of Japanese art—flat areas of strong, unmodulated color bounded by a prominent outline and the decorative juxtaposition of pattern—had attracted artists since the 1860s. The inherently democratic nature of Japanese prints, created expressly to be both appealing and affordable to the common people, also came to be a model to French artists who were themselves without aristocratic patrons and, for a variety of reasons, in search of a broader public.

Although invented by the German Aloys Senefelder, lithography reached its fullest potential in the hands of French artists. As Douglas Druick has indicated, national pride may also have played a role in the revival of original lithography in France during the last decades of the 18th century. The loss of the provinces Alsace and Lorraine to the Germans following France's defeat in the Franco-Prussian war in 1871 was a tremendous blow, and the call for revenge was continuous. This sentiment of national disgrace, Druick argues, was an important factor motivating the intense effort to establish lithography as a naturalized French citizen. Druick suggests that although they were well aware that the accepted date for the invention of lithography was 1796, the French planned the centennial celebration for 1895, expressly to "beat" the German centennial which had been slated for 1896.[8]

Contemporary critics such as Roger-Marx and Jean Lahor had been calling for a renewal of French decorative arts with the goal of creating art for a broader public.[9] The democratic quality of prints as a means of circulating fine art among a wider audience was an integral element in the revival of artistic lithography. André Mellerio, in his synopsis of the movement in 1898, acknowledged these factors in contributing to the popularity of the medium:

> Now it has happened that paintings, statues, and all works that have a value as unique objects by their rarity, have become costly collector's items, accessible only to a limited number. What remains? Prints and original prints. Their artistic value is indisputable. The number of prints that can be pulled, and the reasonableness of price, put them within reach of the general public. And it cannot be denied that besides the big collectors, who sometimes are lovers of art, but often are nothing more than wranglers over expensive objects, either because of vanity, or for hidden speculation, there exists here and now numerous representatives of the middle class who dedicate their leisure time, a portion of their intelligence and their money, to nosing about, to being interested in, and to buying. There is a potential enthusiasm, that could not easily be triggered among ordinary people for this art, that is not yet perfect, but is already more refined. They are beginning to recognize the chromolithograph and to abhor it, preferring the original print.... Little by little, cultivated by efforts of artists, publishers, and magazines, and by the growing culture of a more educated public, this group will become more numerous, with clearer ideas, asking only to see itself encouraged, enlightened, and helped.[10]

Thus, artists made prints—multiples—for greater distribution of their art. Jacques Villon began his career in the midst of this movement, and his color lithograph *La danseuse au Moulin Rouge* (pl. 6) reflects his presence alongside that of Lautrec and the Nabis in Montmartre. Artists applied their talents in lithography to decorate objects as diverse in function as song sheets (figs. 58, 61-63; pls. 57, 59, 60), book jackets (nos. 87, 88, 92, 97; figs. 85, 86, 91, 93-96), birth announcements (fig. 5), and even fans (pl. 98)—in some cases intended not only to be decorative and functional in the conventional sense, but also designed to carry a commercial message.

Pierre Bonnard was one of the first young artists to experiment with the medium of original color lithography in making commercial posters. His *France Champagne*, created in 1891, stimulated Lautrec to try his hand at lithography, resulting in the poster *Au Moulin Rouge—La Goulue*. In 1894 Bonnard designed the poster for the literary and artistic review *La revue blanche* (pl. 27) and in 1897 one for *L'Estampe et l'affiche* (pl. 7), a magazine published by Clément Janin and André Mellerio, devoted to this very topic. Posters were not only a new forum for artistic expression, but also became a new frontier for collectors. Beginning in 1891, Sagot's gallery published a catalogue of the posters it offered for sale. In 1893 an article by T.J. Hiatt, "The Collection of Posters. A New Field for Connoisseurs," stated, "The print collector, wearied for the moment of engravings or etchings, might without loss of dignity, turn his attention to the wall-pictures that gaily decorate the tedious new streets of Paris...."[11] From 1895 on, numerous publications dealing with posters appeared. One of these, *Les maîtres de l'affiche* (1895-1900) was published in several volumes, each of which began with a preface by Roger-Marx, followed by reductions on quality paper of the most admired posters. Thus, collectors and the interested public could examine with great ease the body of new posters being produced and collect the images in this more manageable small format in addition to, or instead of, collecting the enormous posters themselves, including such works as Ibels's *L'Escarmouche* (fig. 12) and Lautrec's *La revue blanche* (no. 13).

Among the periodicals supporting the lithographic revival were *Le courrier français*, which included lithographic reductions of new posters by Chéret as special supplements to its issues beginning in 1890. *La revue blanche*, the artistic and literary review published by the brothers Alexandre and Thadée Natanson, commissioned posters from Bonnard and Lautrec (no. 13; pl. 27) and began to publish lithographic frontispieces by Lautrec and the Nabis in 1893 (figs. 15-24). *L'Escarmouche* (The Skirmish), an illustrated journal published by Georges Darien, appeared in November 1893; although it lasted a brief 10 issues, it sponsored the production of some fine prints. This publisher took an overtly radical approach to his trade by encouraging absolute artistic freedom, echoing contemporary anarchist political cries. In the inaugural issue he wrote, "This newspaper, then, will be the voice of the vanguard fighters—the voice of the sharpshooters whose shots, unconcerned with the password, induce the canon's thunder—the voice of the lone marksmen for liberal opinions."[12] Darien commissioned original lithographs, which he sold as individual prints and also reproduced photomechanically within each issue of the journal. Among the artists who contributed were Hermann-Paul (fig. 33), Bonnard (figs. 8-11), and Ibels.

André Marty, publisher of the *Journal des artistes*, launched the first album of original prints in 1893. The publication, called *L'Estampe originale*, was printed in a limited edition of 100 and issued quarterly for a total of nine installments. Marty, who is portrayed by the artist Willette dashing through the streets of Paris with an album of *L'Estampe originale* under his arm (fig. 70), invited both new and established artists to contribute. In the same year that he launched this publication, Marty invited Ibels and Lautrec to illustrate Georges Montorgueil's text for the book *Le café-concert* (figs. 65-69). Each artist contributed 11 lithographs depicting specific performers and places, and although today Toulouse-Lautrec is better known, in 1893 the honor belonged to Ibels. It was he, therefore, who designed the illustration for the cover of the publication.

Marty's success with *L'Estampe originale* inspired the creation of several subsequent print albums. The artist Maurice Dumont published *L'Epreuve* in 1894-95. It was intended both as a literary periodical and a print album, and among the contributing artists were Puvis de Chavannes, Fantin-Latour, Bonnard (figs. 28, 29), Vuillard, Denis, Felicien Rops, and the little-known Belgian artist Henry de Groux (fig. 30). *L'Estampe moderne*, published from May 1897 to

April 1899, was perhaps the most "democratic" of all print albums of the period. Published in a "limited edition" of 2000, it was issued in inexpensive albums of four prints each. Although it professed to be a publication of original prints, most of the plates were done in a combination of photomechanical techniques and are overtly reproductive in nature. In general, these images lack the freshness and aesthetic quality of even the earlier, lively photomechanical illustrations by Lautrec and others found in journals such as *Le Mirliton* and *Le Rire*. Evenepoel's *Au Square* (pl. 31) is unusual among the prints in *L'Estampe moderne* as an original lithograph of considerable artistic merit.

The birth of the avant-garde theater in the 1890s created opportunities for many young artists to devote their talents to designing covers for playbills. If journal illustration and the designing of posters and other commercial objects represented a popular aspect of artistic activity, the theater enabled young artists to apply their craft to one of the most intellectual movements of the day, namely symbolism. The actor Aurélien Lugné-Poe was a close friend of the Nabis artists—and by extension of Toulouse-Lautrec—and it was through Lugné-Poe that these artists, in particular, became closely involved with the theater. Vuillard, with the help of Lugné-Poe, received the commission to design one cover in 1890 for Antoine's naturalist Théâtre Libre (fig. 41). Later, when Lugné-Poe performed with Paul Fort's Théâtre d'Art, images by many of the Nabis decorated programs for these presentations and were reproduced in the *Livre d'art*, a periodical published by the theater. One example is Bonnard's *Le geste du roy*, which decorated a program cover and was also reproduced as an illustration in the *Livre d'art* (fig. 39). When Lugné-Poe founded his own symbolist Théâtre de l'Oeuvre in 1893, his friends collaborated in the design of sets, costumes, and program covers. In programs such as Vuillard's for *Un ennemi du peuple* (fig. 45) and *Rosmersholm* (fig. 44), text is thoroughly integrated into the composition. In keeping with a symbolist presentation, the ambiguous atmosphere and dramatic contrast of black and white in these images evoke rather than describe the content of the play.[13] Lautrec created three program covers for the Théâtre de l'Oeuvre, among them one for *Le chariot de terre cuite* in 1895, on which he depicted the literary critic Félix Fénéon riding an elephant (fig. 46).

The wide and varied range of new patronage cultivated by artists in the 1890s was surely one of the factors contributing to the rich diversity of artistic production. Wealthy aristocrats and the church were replaced by the bourgeoisie, publishers of journals and books, and product manufacturers as well as figures involved in the theater and *café-concert*. This climate helped to create the demand for new kinds of art, and these challenges were met with the inventiveness and boldness necessary to unite a generation's new aesthetic language with a new technology for its communication.

Patricia Eckert Boyer

Notes

[1]See Henri Perruchot, *Toulouse-Lautrec*, trans. Humphrey Ware, New York, 1962, p. 157.

[2]Phillip Dennis Cate and Patricia Eckert Boyer, *The Circle of Toulouse-Lautrec*, New Brunswick, N.J., 1986, p. 17.

[3]Cate and Boyer, p. 19.

[4]See, for example, *Au Moulin Rouge—La Goulue*, 1891 (Wolfgang Wittrock, *Toulouse-Lautrec: The Complete Prints*, London, 1985, vol. 1, p. 1); *L'Anglais au Moulin Rouge: M. Warner*, 1892 (Wittrock, p. 2); *Au Pied de l'echafaud*, 1893 (Delteil, p. 347).

[5]See Phillip Dennis Cate, "The Popularization of Lautrec," in Riva Castleman and Wolfgang Wittrock, eds., *Henri de Toulouse-Lautrec: Images of the 1890s*, New York, 1985, p. 77.

[6]André Mellerio, *La lithographie originale en couleurs*, Paris, 1898, p. 6, translated by Margaret Needham in Phillip Dennis Cate and Sinclair Hitchings, *The Color Revolution*, New Brunswick, N.J., 1978, p. 81.

[7]Roger-Marx, *La décoration et l'art industriel à l'Exposition Universelle de 1889*, Paris, 1890, p. 36. In calling Chéret a *décorateur*, Roger-Marx is referring to Chéret's application of original art to functional, non-elite objects such as his commercial placards, which decorated the streets of Paris.

[8]Douglas Druick and Peter Zegers, *La Pierre Parle: Lithography in France 1848-1900*, Ottawa, 1981, p. 94.

[9]See, for example, Roger-Marx, pp. 35-36, and Jean Lahor, *L'Art nouveau*, Paris, 1901, pp. 1-3.

[10]Mellerio, translated in Cate and Hitchings, p. 81.

[11]Charles T.J. Hiatt, "The Collecting of Posters. A New Field for Connoisseurs," *The Studio* 1 (May 1893), pp. 61-64. The "tedious" streets referred to were the wide boulevards designed by Baron Haussmann that stimulated the poster movement by offering a more open vista by which the passerby could have a better view of placards on the walls of the buildings.

[12]*L'Escarmouche*, [November 13] 1893.

[13]On the Nabis' illustration of programs for the symbolist theater, see Elizabeth Prelinger, "The Art of the Nabis: From Symbolism to Modernism," in Patricia Eckert Boyer and Elizabeth Prelinger, *The Nabis and the Parisian Avant-Garde*, New Brunswick, N.J., 1988, pp. 96-98.

Catalogue of the Exhibition

This catalogue was prepared by Erwin Raible and edited by Catherine L. O'Hara with the participation of art history seminar students led by Professor Lloyd Engelbrecht at the University of Cincinnati.

Henri Marie-Raymond de Toulouse-Lautrec Monfa was born November 24, 1864, at his family's château, the Hôtel du Bosc, in Albi, France. His father, Comte Alphonse de Toulouse-Lautrec Monfa, and his mother, Viscomtesse Adèle Zoë Tapié de Céleyran, were first cousins. The inbreeding of generations finally manifested itself in their son, causing him physical problems that were to plague him for his entire life.

In 1872, the family moved to the Hôtel Perey in Paris where Toulouse-Lautrec attended the Lycée Fontanes (later the Lycée Condorcet); he was noted as a brilliant scholar. There, he met his lifelong friend and primary biographer, Maurice Joyant. The following year, he met his father's close friend the artist René Princeteau and his associates John Lewis Brown and Jean-Louis Forain, all of whom were to influence his work. Shortly thereafter Toulouse-Lautrec left the Lycée Fontanes and Paris because of poor health and returned to Albi where he resumed his education with tutors.

On May 30, 1878, while getting up from a chair in the dining room of the Hôtel du Bosc, Toulouse-Lautrec fell on the slippery floor and broke his left leg. Complications in healing led to long-term incapacitation, which in turn led Toulouse-Lautrec to begin drawing and painting seriously. While continuing his recuperation at a spa in Barèges in August 1879, he broke his right leg. Toulouse-Lautrec's earliest landscapes were produced at Albi and the family estate during his recuperation in 1880. At this same time, Bastille Day, July 14, 1880, was considered to be the beginning of the *belle époque,* an era that he ultimately would come to epitomize more than any other group or individual.

On his return to Paris in 1881, Toulouse-Lautrec began his formal art training under Princeteau's direction. Later that year in November he received his baccalaureate. In March 1882 he entered Bonnat's studio, moving on to Cormon's in 1883. Around this time Toulouse-Lautrec became strongly influenced by Japanese prints, having seen them in their first important Western show at the Galerie Georges Petit. Later that year he rented his first studio in Montmartre.

Toulouse-Lautrec met his idol, Degas, in 1885 and was to become lifelong friends with cabaret performer Aristide Bruant following the opening of his cabaret, Le Mirliton. In 1886 he met van Gogh shortly before leaving Cormon's studio to devote his life to painting and Montmartre and before van Gogh left for the South of France at Toulouse-Lautrec's suggestion. That year he produced his first magazine illustration for *Le courrier français* (fig. 73) and his first color illustration for *Le Mirliton.*

The Société des XX (later called La Libre Esthétique) invited Toulouse-Lautrec to exhibit in 1888. He exhibited with the Nabis at the first Salon des Indépendants and later at the first Le Barc de Boutteville show. Although he was not a member of the Nabis, he was closely associated with them through *La revue blanche* and his theater affiliations.

Probably the most important event of 1889 for Toulouse-Lautrec was the October 5 opening of the Moulin Rouge with which he was to become inextricably associated during its heyday. Toulouse-Lautrec also sold his first painting that year. Influenced strongly by Bonnard's *France Champagne* poster in early 1891, Toulouse-Lautrec produced his late-1891 poster for the Moulin Rouge, revolutionizing poster design for all time.

In 1893 Toulouse-Lautrec was offered his first one-man show at the Galerie Boussod Valadon. During the following years, he produced numerous posters, illustrations, and other printed designs.

By 1897 Toulouse-Lautrec began to be plagued by serious signs of mental and physical deterioration; yet, he continued to produce prints, drawings, and paintings. His most important suite of color lithographs, the *Elles* album was published by Gustave Pellet during this period. His deterioration continued until February 1899, when his mother had him confined to the sanatorium at Neuilly where he was to remain until May 17 of that year. After his release, he continued to deteriorate and work until July 1901 when he was forced to leave Paris, returning once again to the safety of his mother in the South of France where he died at her Malromé estate on September 9.

Edouard Vuillard was born November 11, 1868, at Cuiseaux, Saône-et-Loire, France. His father was a retired colonial army officer with the Legion of Honor and 27 years older than his mother, Marie (née Michaud), daughter of a textile designer and manufacturer. Edouard was the youngest of three children.

In 1877 the family moved to Paris where young Vuillard began his studies at the Marist École Rocroy. His father died in 1883, and his mother set up business as a dress and corset maker in their apartment on the rue Daunou. By 1884 Vuillard had entered the Lycée Condorcet on scholarship, and there he first met Ker-Xavier Roussel, Maurice Denis, Aurélien Lugné-Poe, and Thadée and Alexandre Natanson as fellow students. They were all to play important roles in Vuillard's life from that time forward. In 1886 while attending the military college École St.-Cyr, Vuillard and Roussel were also attending day classes at Delacroix's studio on the Place Furstemberg and evening classes at the École des Gobelins, both taught by Prix de Rome winner Diogène Maillart. It was during this time that Vuillard decided to devote his life to painting and at the insistence of Roussel entered the École des Beaux-Arts, for a short time studying under Jean-Léon Gérome.

In 1888 Vuillard and Roussel enrolled in the Académie Julian where Pierre Bonnard, Denis, Henri-Gabriel Ibels, Félix Vallotton, Paul Ranson, and Paul Sérusier were students. Shortly thereafter in 1889, Sérusier returned to the Académie Julian from working with Gauguin in Pont-Aven and formed the group known as the Nabis—from the Hebrew word for prophet—based on the theories and techniques passed on to him by Gauguin. Vuillard became *le Nabis "le Zouave."* Reinforcement of Gauguin's theories came later that year for the young Nabis during an exhibition of works by Gauguin, Émile Bernard, Charles Laval, and others under the name of Peintres Synthétistes et Symbolistes held at the Café Volpini during the Paris Universal Exposition.

In 1890 while sharing a studio with Bonnard, Denis, and Lugné-Poe, Vuillard received his first commission to create a theater program for the Théâtre Libre through Lugné-Poe. This was the beginning of his extensive relationship with the theater, which included additional programs as well as designs for sets and costumes for the Théâtre Libre, Paul Fort's Théâtre d'Art, and Lugné-Poe's Théâtre de l'Ouevre, which Vuillard named.

Vuillard participated in the first Nabis exhibition at Le Barc de Boutteville in 1891 and that same year had his first solo exhibition at the offices of *La revue blanche,* where notice of his work was taken by art critics Gustave Geffroy, Claude Roger-Marx, Arsène Alexandre, and Albert Aurier. Through *La revue blanche* Vuillard met Toulouse-Lautrec and subsequently began his lithographic experiments at Ancourt. The following year Vuillard exhibited with the Nabis at the Salon des Indépendants and at the second and third Le Barc de Boutteville shows. In 1896, he, along with Bonnard and Toulouse-Lautrec, was invited to exhibit at the prestigious La Libre Esthétique in Brussels.

In 1893 Vuillard's sister, Marie, married Roussel. That year, he created his first lithographic frontispiece, *Intérieur,* for *La revue blanche* (fig. 15) and illustrated the frontispiece for Maurice Beaubourg's *Nouvelles passionnées* (fig. 96). He designed his first and only poster for Becane, a meat-juice tonic for sports enthusiasts, in 1894.

By 1898 Vuillard's contribution to the lithographi revolution of the 1890s was cause for his being featured in André Mellerio's landmark book *La lithographie originale en couleurs.* This doubtless prompted Ambroise Vollard to publish Vuillard's suite of color lithographs *Paysages et intérieurs* in 1899.

Following the turn of the century, Vuillard's print production slowed considerably with only periodic pieces produced as book illustrations. Paint became his favored medium, and his paintings reflect the socially fashionable world in which his commissions now allowed him to move. His earlier intimate interiors featuring quotidian portraits of his family were now replaced by ostentatious settings serving as backdrops for their socially prominent inhabitants.

Threatened by the German advance in 1940, Vuillard begrudgingly left Paris only to die a short time later on June 21 at La Baule.

Pierre Bonnard was born October 30, 1867, at Fontenay-aux-Roses, a suburb of Paris, the second son of Eugène Bonnard, *chef de bureau* at the Ministry of War, and his wife Elisabeth, called Elise (née Mertzdorff), of Alsace. By 1877 Bonnard was attending boarding school and soon began his classical education, first at the Lycée Vanves, then at the Lycée Louis LeGrand, and finally at the Lycée Charlemagne in Paris. An excellent student, he received his baccalaureate and faculty of law and in 1887 his law degree. Later that year he began studies at the École des Beaux-Arts and the Académie Julian where he met Vuillard, Roussel, Ibels, Denis, Ranson, Vallotton, and Sérusier.

Bonnard began working for the assistant public prosecutor after having failed the Prix de Rome and the civil service competition in 1889. During this period he decided to devote his life to painting and rented his first studio in the Batignolles quarter. As may be expected, Bonnard was one of the original Nabis when the group formed that year and was known as *le Nabis très japonard*. Shortly thereafter Bonnard received his first major commission and sold his first poster design to France Champagne for 100 francs. The poster was a huge success on the streets of Paris and led to Bonnard's meeting Toulouse-Lautrec.

In 1890 Bonnard shared an apartment/studio with Vuillard, Denis, and the actor Lugné-Poe at 28 rue Pigalle. Bonnard's sister, Andrée, married the young composer Claude Terrasse that year, thus initiating a productive music illustration career for her brother.

Bonnard exhibited with the Nabis at the first Le Barc de Boutteville show and became affiliated with *La revue blanche*. By 1892 art critics Roger-Marx and Gustave Geffroy began to acknowledge Bonnard and his work, having become acquainted with him through Vuillard. Bonnard exhibited with the Nabis at the Salon des Indépendants and collaborated with Toulouse-Lautrec on Victor Joze's novel *Reine de joie* (figs. 91, 91A).

In 1894, Maria Boursin (Marthe) became Bonnard's favorite model; they married in 1925. Marthe may have been the model who posed for Bonnard's 1894 poster for *La revue blanche* (pl. 27). Bonnard, Vuillard, Ibels, Vallotton, and Toulouse-Lautrec were commissioned to work in a new medium that year—stained glass—by Samuel Bing of the Maison de l'Art Nouveau. Their windows were produced by Tiffany and Company of New York.

The 1896 founding of the Théâtre des Pantins came about as a collaboration between Bonnard, Vuillard, Terrasse, Franc Nohain, and Alfred Jarry. Bonnard had his first one-man show that year at the Galerie Durand-Ruel and exhibited at the last Le Barc de Boutteville show to include the Nabis as a group. Although invited to exhibit in 1896 at La Libre Esthétique, he did not do so until 1897. The following year the Nabis had their first exhibition at the Galerie Vollard, and Vollard published Bonnard's suite of color lithographs, *Aspects of Parisian Life*. Following Vollard's lead, the Galerie Durand-Ruel, in a "Tribute to Redon," organized a landmark exhibition of the Nabis in 1899.

Bonnard's involvement in the lithographic revolution garnered him attention in Mellerio's *La lithographie originale en couleurs* of 1898 as well as the commission for the cover and the frontispiece (figs. 1-3). He went on to illustrate a number of books and to create prints and posters throughout his life. Bonnard died January 23, 1947, at his villa, Le Bosquet, at Le Cannet in the South of France.

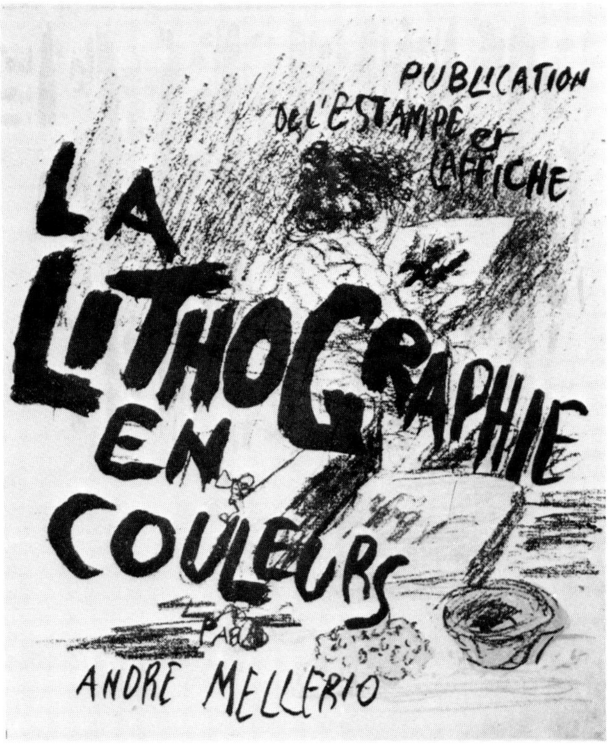

1

1.* Pierre Bonnard
La lithographie originale en couleurs
Book cover, 1898
Lithograph printed in three colors
h. 21.5 x w. 19.5 cm.

André Mellerio, patron and documenter of print making, produced a record of nearly a decade of avant-garde print making with the May 1898 appearance of his book *La lithographie originale en couleurs* published by Edward Pelletan of *L'Estampe et l'affiche. La lithographie originale en couleurs* was to encourage the further development of color lithography. It explained the lithographic process and featured short sketches on the most prominent artists with their specific involvement in and contributions to the field. Bonnard, Vuillard, Toulouse-Lautrec, Ibels, and Chéret among others were discussed at length. It also included information on additional printers, publishers, and publications.

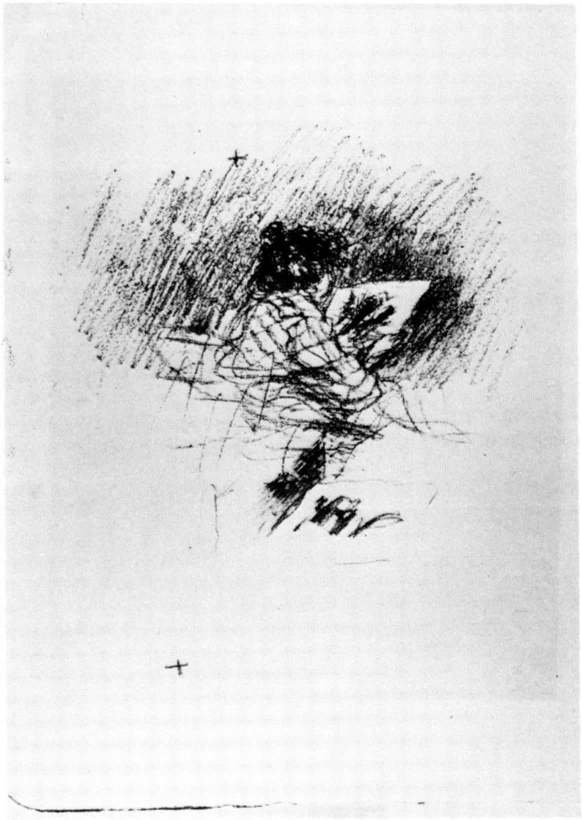

2

2.* Pierre Bonnard
Proof for cover of ***La lithographie originale en couleurs,*** 1898
Lithograph printed in dark gray
h. 21.5 x w. 18.5 cm.

3.** Pierre Bonnard
La loge
Frontispiece for ***La lithographie originale en couleurs,*** 1898
Lithographic proof printed in four colors
h. 21 x w. 19 cm.

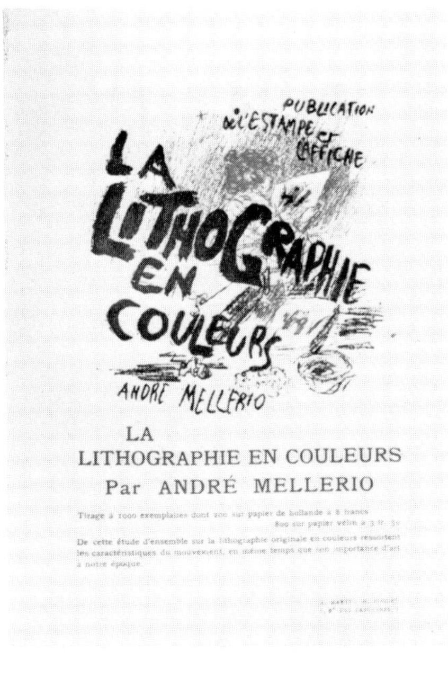
LA
LITHOGRAPHIE EN COULEURS
Par ANDRÉ MELLERIO

4

***Illustrated**
****Color plate**

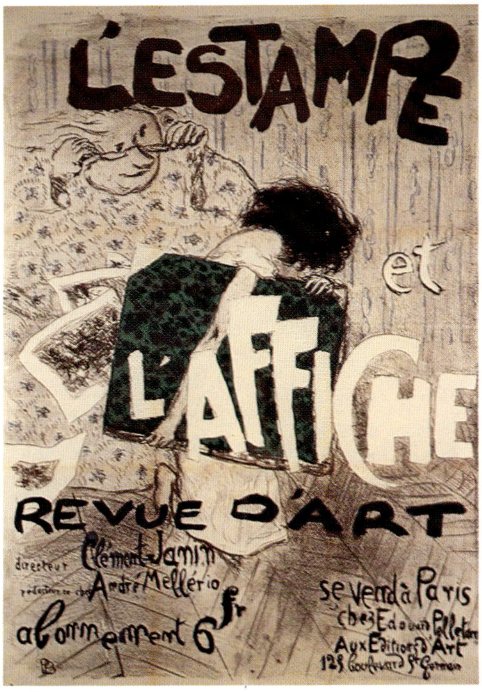
L'ESTAMPE
et
L'AFFICHE
REVUE D'ART
directeur Clément-Janin
André Mellerio
abonnement 6 fr
se vend à Paris
chez Edouard Pelletan
Aux Editions d'Art
125 Boulevard St Germain

7

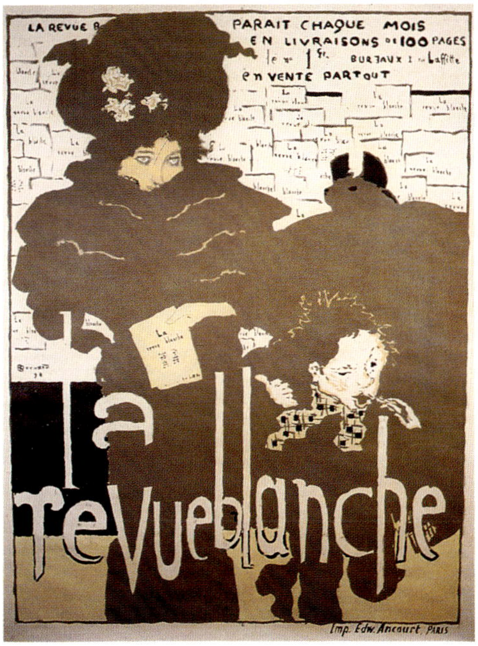
PARAIT CHAQUE MOIS
EN LIVRAISONS DE 100 PAGES
EN VENTE PARTOUT
La revue blanche
Imp. Edw. Ancourt, PARIS

27

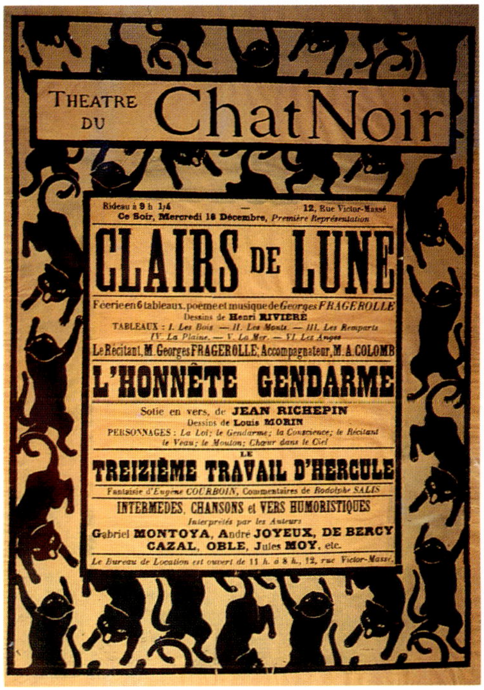
THEATRE DU Chat Noir
Rideau à 9 h 1/4 — 12, Rue Victor-Massé
Ce Soir, Mercredi 18 Décembre, Première Représentation
CLAIRS DE LUNE
Féerie en 6 tableaux, poème et musique de Georges FRAGEROLLE
Dessins de Henri RIVIÈRE
TABLEAUX : I. Les Bois — II. Les Monts. — III. Les Remparts
IV. La Plaine. — V. La Mer. — VI. Les Anges
Le Récitant, M. Georges FRAGEROLLE; Accompagnateur, M. A. COLOMB
L'HONNÊTE GENDARME
Sotie en vers, de JEAN RICHEPIN
Dessins de Louis MORIN
PERSONNAGES : La Loi; le Gendarme; la Conscience; le Récitant
le Veau; le Mouton; Chœur dans le Ciel
LE
TREIZIÈME TRAVAIL D'HERCULE
Fantaisie d'Eugène COURBOIN, Commentaires de Rodolphe SALIS
INTERMEDES, CHANSONS et VERS HUMORISTIQUES
Interprétés par les Auteurs
Gabriel MONTOYA, André JOYEUX, DE BERCY
CAZAL, OBLE, Jules MOY, etc.
Le Bureau de Location est ouvert de 11 h. à 8 h., 12, rue Victor-Massé.

50

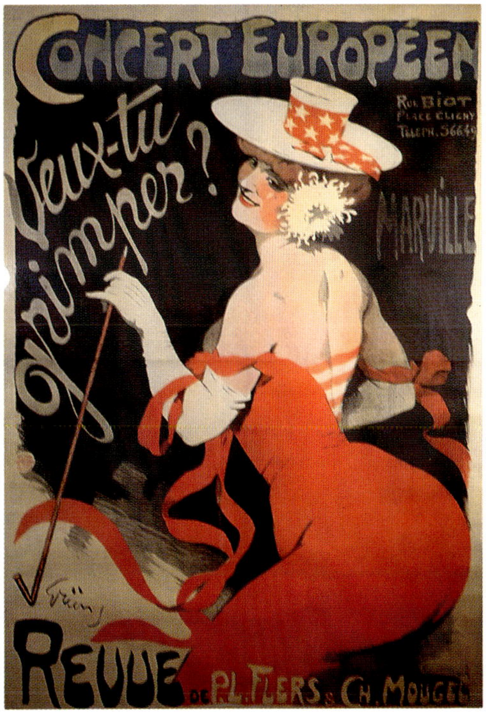
CONCERT EUROPÉEN
Rue BIOT
PLACE CLICHY
Veux-tu grimper?
MARVILLE
REVUE DE PL. FLERS & CH. MOUGEL

64

4.* Pierre Bonnard
Advertisement for ***La lithographie originale en couleurs,*** 1898
Photomechanical print in three colors
h. 16.5 x w. 10.5 cm.

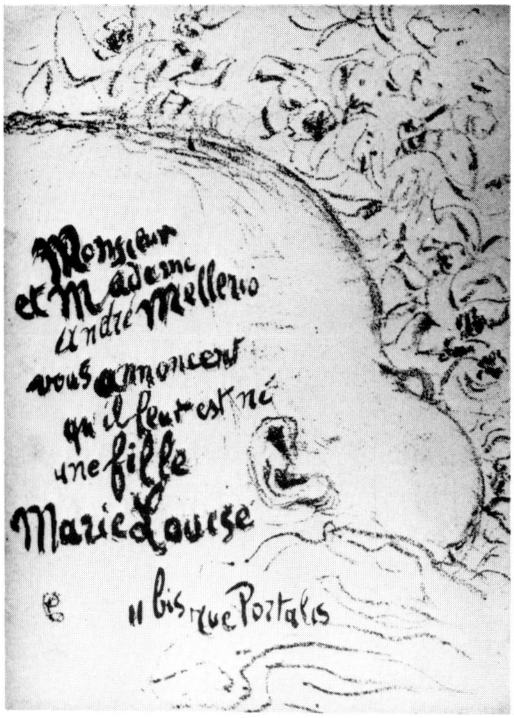

5

5.* Pierre Bonnard
Birth Announcement, 1898
Lithograph printed in rose
h. 15.8 x w. 12 cm.

Bonnard designed this birth announcement for André Mellerio's daughter Marie-Louise.

6.** Jacques Gaston Duchamp Villon
La danseuse au Moulin Rouge
Published by ***L'Estampe et l'affiche,*** 1899
Lithograph printed in five colors
h. 28.8 x w. 21 cm.

Jacques Villon was born in Deauville in 1875. By 1894 he had enrolled in the École des Beaux-Arts in Paris as a student of Cormon, working in the style of Toulouse-Lautrec and Théophile-Alexandre Steinlen. Influence by the fauves and cubists moved him into abstraction early on and the subsequent founding of his own studio in Bordeaux. Villon died in Puteaux, France, in June 1963.

7.** Pierre Bonnard
Poster for ***L'Estampe et l'affiche,*** 1897
Lithograph printed in three colors
h. 80 x w. 60 cm.

This poster advertised the biweekly journal *L'Estampe et l'affiche* published by André Mellerio and edited by Clément Janin from March 1897 through December 1899. The publication was based on the policy that color lithography was the special artistic form of the time, and it promoted the opinion that the print and the poster were comparable art forms. Therefore, it documented in detail the prints and posters published by specific dealers, printers, and individual artists and published regular lists of current prices and edition sizes. It discussed and critiqued exhibitions and presented feature articles on artists and printing techniques.

L'Estampe et l'affiche included this poster by Bonnard as well as one by Peské and prints by Odilon Redon, Henri Fantin-Latour, Denis, Villon (pl. 6), and others.

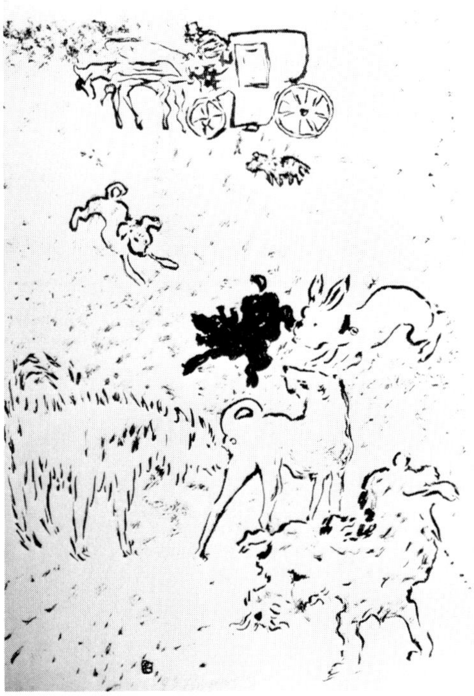

8

8.* Pierre Bonnard
Les chiens
Published for ***L'Escarmouche*** 5,
December 10, 1893
Pencil-signed lithograph printed in brownish-black
h. 38.2 x w. 27.7 cm.

L'Escarmouche (The Skirmish) was a short-lived, weekly publication begun by novelist and journalist Georges Darien, a leading figure in the anarchist movement whose views were set down in his book *La voleur.* Toulouse-Lautrec encouraged the founding of *L'Escarmouche,* which strove to produce three new designs by contemporary artists in each issue. Unfortunately only 10 issues were published between November 12, 1893, and January 14, 1894. There were 12 designs by Toulouse-Lautrec, six each by Ibels and Hermann-Paul, one each by Vallotton and Louis Anquetin, and four by Bonnard (figs. 9-11). Besides the production of photomechanical designs, *L'Escarmouche* published single-sheet lithographs in editions of 100, most of which are signed and numbered and were sold through the publisher and art dealer Kleinmann for 2.50 francs each.

9.* Pierre Bonnard
Garde municipal
Published for ***L'Escarmouche*** 8,
December 31, 1893
Pencil-signed lithograph printed in brownish-black
h. 25.5 x w. 16.5 cm.

10.* Pierre Bonnard
Jeune femme aux bas noirs/Dans intimité
Published for ***L'Escarmouche*** 2,
January 14, 1894
Pencil-signed lithograph printed in brownish-black
h. 29 x w. 12.7 cm.

11.* Pierre Bonnard
Conversation
Intended for publication in ***L'Escarmouche,*** 1893
Pencil-signed lithograph printed in brownish-black
h. 29.5 x w. 25 cm.

12.* Henri-Gabriel Ibels
L'Escarmouche
Published by ***Les maîtres de l'affiche,*** 1896
Lithograph printed in four colors
h. 26.1 x w. 19.9 cm.

Henri-Gabriel Ibels was born in Paris November 30, 1867, of Dutch origin. He first met Bonnard and Vuillard at the Académie Julian and was an original member of the Nabis, known as *le Nabis journaliste* because of his involvement with numerous publications.

Ibels portrayed the work and leisure activities of ordinary people. His association with the anarchist movement frequently appeared as social commentary in his work. In 1898 he founded the illustrated pro-Dreyfus publication *Le sifflet.* This 1893 poster for *L'Escarmouche* portrays Ibels's typical working-class types. The café shown was a popular left-bank, anarchist gathering spot located on the Place Maubert and can be seen in numerous works by Ibels. Yet another example of his working-class type can be seen in the lithograph *Paysanne au panier* produced for *La revue blanche* (fig. 24).

Ibels died in Paris in 1936.

From 1896 through 1900 *Les maîtres de l'affiche* was produced by Chaix, the printing house under the art direction of Jules Chéret, who was almost solely responsible for the triumph of the commercial poster:

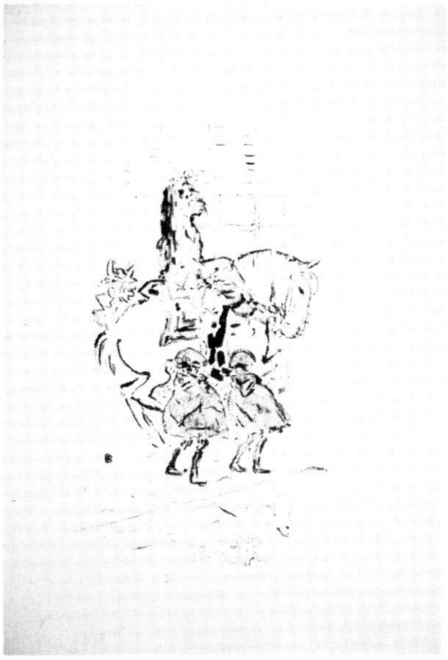

9

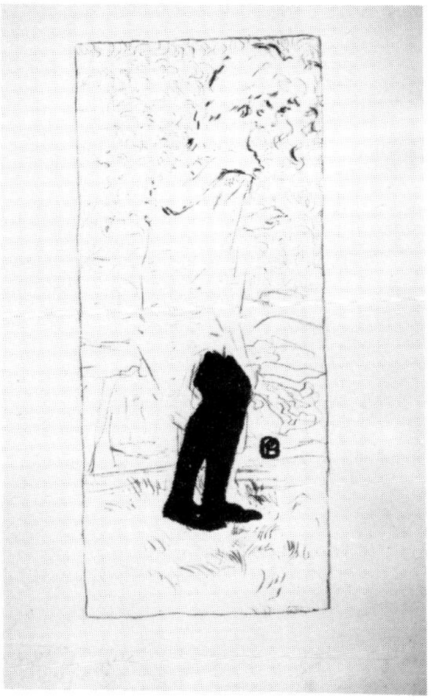

10

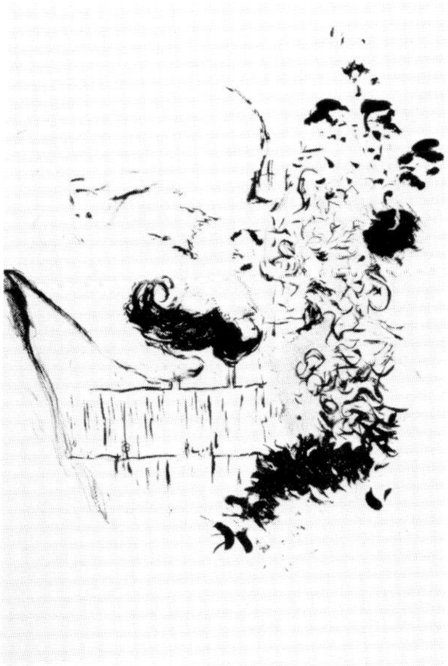

11

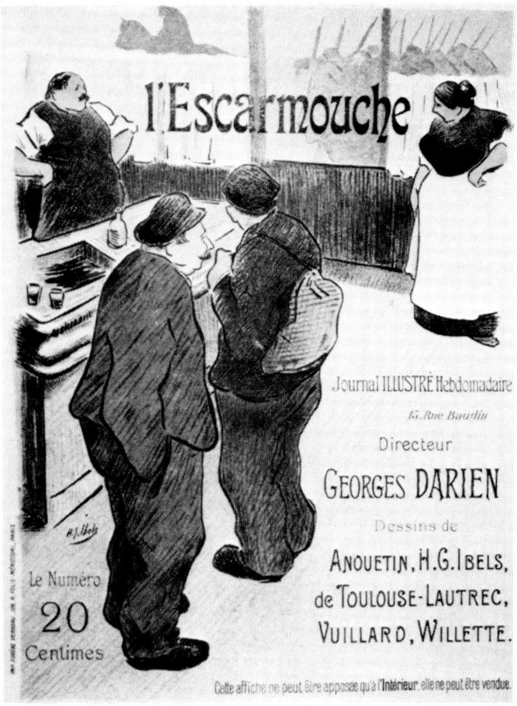

12

Les maîtres de l'affiche was something of a self-tribute.

As a collection of posters or large prints proved difficult to store, the logical consequence of the vogue for this artistic means of expression was hand-drawn reductions. Of the four "posters" lithographically produced on quality papers in each monthly installment, one was always by Chéret himself, making 60 in all. Other French artists accounted for half of the prints, and the 60 remaining were by foreign artists. In addition, there were 16 supplemental drawings. The text for *Les maîtres de l'affiche* was written by Roger-Marx. Similar publications were produced by others: Maindron published *Les affiches illustrées* in 1896 and *Les affiches étrangères* in 1897; Léon Maillard's 1898 *Les menus et programmes illustrés* was published by Bondet.

13. Henri de Toulouse-Lautrec
La revue blanche
Published by ***Les maîtres de l'affiche,*** 1897
Lithograph printed in four colors
h. 28.5 x w. 19.8 cm.

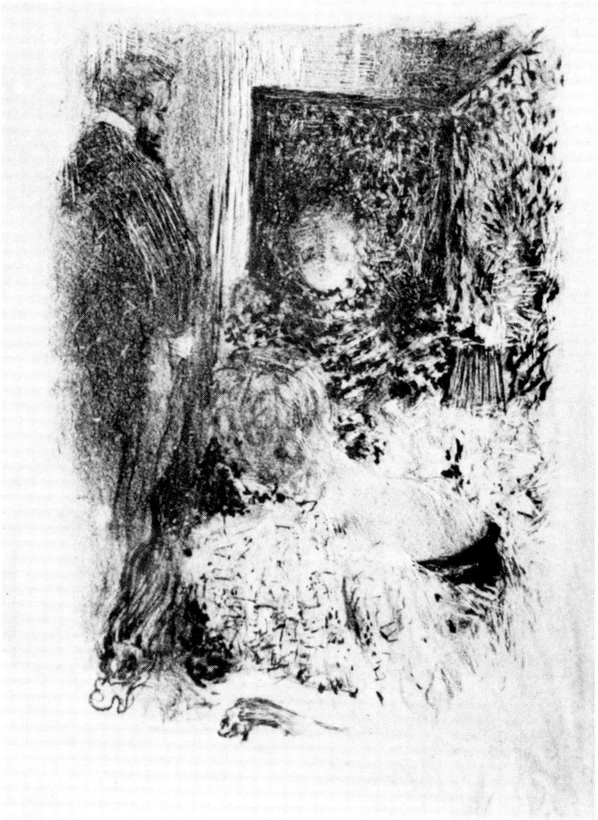

14

14.* Edouard Vuillard
Intimité, 1895
Pencil-signed lithographic proof printed in black
h. 26 x w. 19 cm.

On December 1, 1889, *La revue blanche* made its first appearance in Paris. It was founded during a summer vacation in Belgium in 1889 by Joe Högge, Auguste Jeunehomme, and the Leclercq brothers, Charles and Paul. "White" symbolized an amalgamation of all shades of opinion, just as white is the product of all the colors of the spectrum. Although *La revue blanche* was always edited in Paris, it was printed in Liège, Belgium, until October 15, 1891, when offices were established at 19 rue des Martyrs and the first "all Paris" issues began to appear.

The brothers Thadée and Alexandre Natanson were involved with the review from the outset, and in 1891 they, along with Paul Leclercq, took control of it. The Natanson takeover seems to have occurred without resistance. The new regime had the energy, intelligence, and finances necessary for the journal to survive and prosper. It was, however, Misia Natanson, the captivating and musically and intellectually gifted wife of Thadée, around whom the literary and artistic figures of *La revue blanche* revolved. She was to begin the most celebrated avant-garde Parisian salon while still in her twenties. Misia was the "muse" of *La revue blanche*.

The publication itself was politically left-wing and featured avant-garde fiction and illustrations as well as articles on theater, music, and sports. Contributors included Ibsen, Stendahl, Strindberg, Chekov, Tolstoy, Jarry, Verlaine, Gide, and Wilde. Over 40 artists had their work published or reproduced by *La revue blanche,* including Bonnard, Vuillard, Rippl-Rónai, Toulouse-Lautrec, Vallotton, Denis, Sérusier, Roussel, Munch, Whistler, Gauguin, Redon, and Ibels.

Bonnard and Toulouse-Lautrec produced posters for *La revue blanche* in 1894 and 1897, respectively (no. 13; pl. 27). In 1895 the *Album de la revue blanche* was produced by L'Estampe Original and contained reprints of 12 lithographs that had been published in *La revue blanche* between July 1893 and December 1894. *La revue blanche* also published numerous illustrated books by the various artists and writers associated with the journal. Because of financial difficulties, it ceased publication in April 1903.

In this lithograph, the standing figure to the left is Thadée Natanson. Misia, with her back to us, is seated in the foreground. A cat is in the lower left, and an unidentified female figure appears in the doorway.

15.* Edouard Vuillard
Intérieur
Published in ***La revue blanche,*** 1893
Lithograph printed in black
h. 19 x w. 12 cm.

This, Vuillard's first lithograph for *La revue blanche,* appeared in the July 1893 issue.

16.* Pierre Bonnard
Femme au parapluie
Published in ***La revue blanche,*** 1895
Lithograph printed in two colors
h. 25 x w. 15.5 cm.

17.* Henri de Toulouse-Lautrec
Carnaval
Published in ***La revue blanche,*** 1894
Lithograph printed in two colors
h. 24.6 x w. 16.2

18.* Edouard Vuillard
La couturière
Published in ***L'Album de la revue blanche,*** 1895
Lithograph printed in two colors
h. 25 x w. 16.5 cm.

19.* Ker-Xavier Roussel
Causerie au jardin
Published in ***La revue blanche,*** 1893
Lithograph printed in black
h. 17.8 x w. 8.4 cm.

Ker-Xavier Roussel was born December 10, 1867, at Lorry-les-Metz, the son of a prestigious doctor. He began his studies in 1876 at the Lycée Condorcet. In 1885 he entered the studio of Diogène Maillart. He later attended the Académie Julian and in the late spring of 1889 became an original member of the Nabis group. In July 1893 he married Vuillard's sister, Marie. After 1900 Roussel primarily devoted himself to the painting of classically inspired mythological scenes of sensual and hedonistic attitude. He died June 6, 1944, at L'Etang-la-Ville.

20.* Pierre Bonnard
Parisiennes
Published in ***La revue blanche,*** 1895
Lithograph printed in black
h. 21.5 x w. 13 cm.

21.* József Rippl-Rónai
Femme et lampe
Published in ***La revue blanche,*** 1895
Lithograph printed in three colors
h. 19.5 x w. 15 cm.

József Rippl-Rónai was born May 24, 1861, in Hungary. After studying fine arts and working in Munich, he came to Paris in 1890. Rippl-Rónai began working in the Nabis manner after an 1889 visit with Gauguin and Émile Bernard in Pont-Aven. By 1891 he was associated with the Nabis and Toulouse-Lautrec through *La revue blanche* and the Théâtre de l'Oeuvre. By 1894 he was officially part of the Nabis group. Rippl-Rónai was one of the major voices relaying ideas and theories from Gauguin to the Nabis by continued contact with the Pont-Aven artists.

22.* Félix Vallotton
Les trois baigneuses
Published in ***La revue blanche,*** 1894
Woodcut printed in black
h. 18.3 x w. 11.2 cm.

Born in 1865 in Lausanne, Switzerland, Vallotton came to Paris and began his studies in 1882 at the École des Beaux-Arts under Jules Lefèbvre. By 1883 he had exhibited at the Salon. By 1890 Vallotton was a student at the Académie Julian and, with Charles Maurin as his mentor, learned the techniques involved in woodcuts, which Maurin had learned from Gauguin and Bernard. Vallotton specialized in woodcuts between 1890 and 1900.

Although not an original member of the Nabis, Vallotton's contact with them, possibly through Toulouse-Lautrec, led him to give up his earlier academic style and develop his enthusiasm for decoration, print making, and poster and magazine illustration. Yet, he always aimed for strength and clarity of form, shying away from symbolism. The juxtaposition of the strong black silhouetted forms on the white ground of his woodcuts often translated into the decorative abstract forms associated with the Nabis and the compositional devices of the shadow theater. He was known, however, as the "foreign Nabis."

Vallotton's interest in the often rude and violent portrayal of contemporary subject matter places him closer to the sensibilities of Toulouse-Lautrec than to the Nabis. Like Ibels, his sympathy with the anarchist movement frequently spawned social and political commentary within his work.

By 1900 Vallotton began a return to his earlier academic style, developing a precise realism in his painting and abandoning his woodcuts almost entirely. He died December 28, 1925, in Paris.

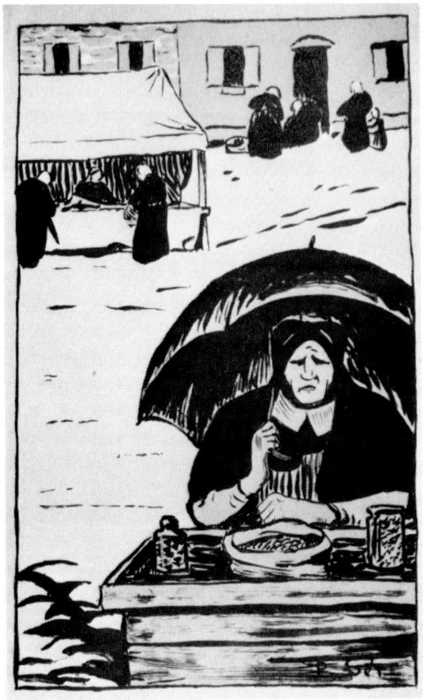

23

23.* Paul Sérusier
La marchande de bonbons au marché breton
Published in ***La revue blanche,*** 1894
Lithograph printed in two colors
h. 22.5 x w. 13.7 cm.

Paul Sérusier was born in Paris in 1863. He was noted as a brilliant student at the Lycée Condorcet and later entered the Académie Julian where he continued as an outstanding student and was student head of the studio. In 1888 Sérusier worked with Gauguin at Pont-Aven, and that fall he returned to Paris and the Académie Julian where he founded the Nabis group, based on the artistic ideas and theories he had discovered in Gauguin's work at Pont-Aven and grounded in the French symbolist and English pre-Raphaelite movements. *The Talisman,* a painting of the Bois d'Amour on the lid of a cigar box, an abstract landscape in bold color painted by Sérusier under Gauguin's guidance, served as the point of departure for the Nabis to question the theories and techniques that they were currently being taught at the Académie Julian. The Nabis' revelation was that color and form have expression independent of subject matter.

Sérusier died in 1927.

24.* Henri-Gabriel Ibels
Paysanne au panier
Published in ***La revue blanche,*** 1894
Lithograph printed in two colors
h. 24 x w. 15.2 cm.

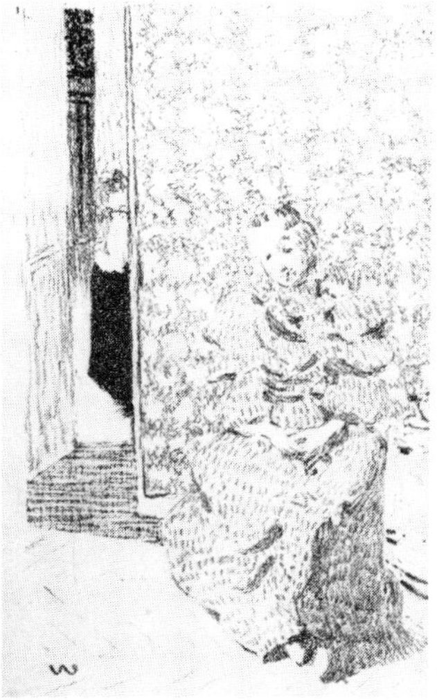
15

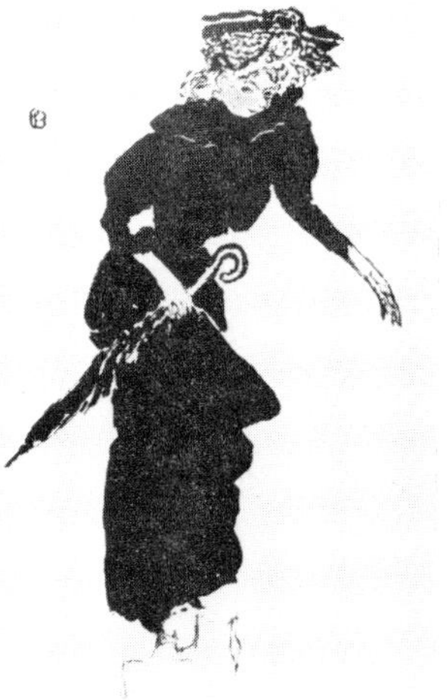
16

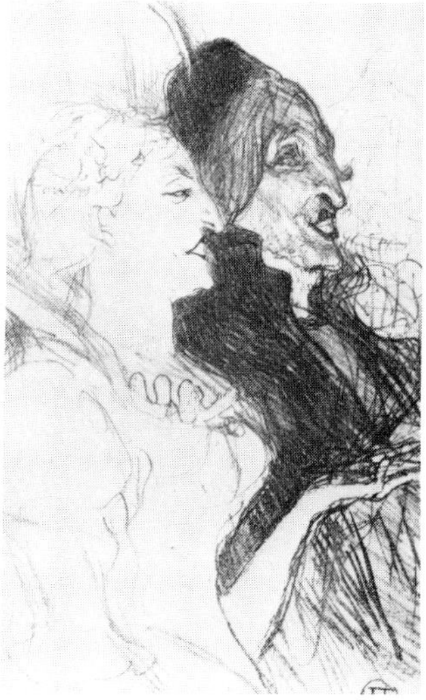
17

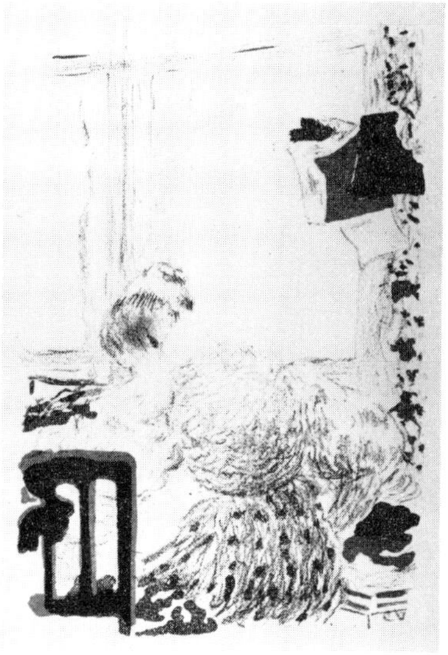
18

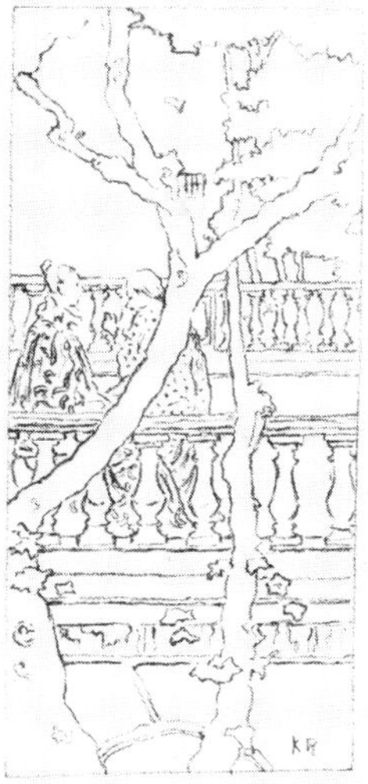
19

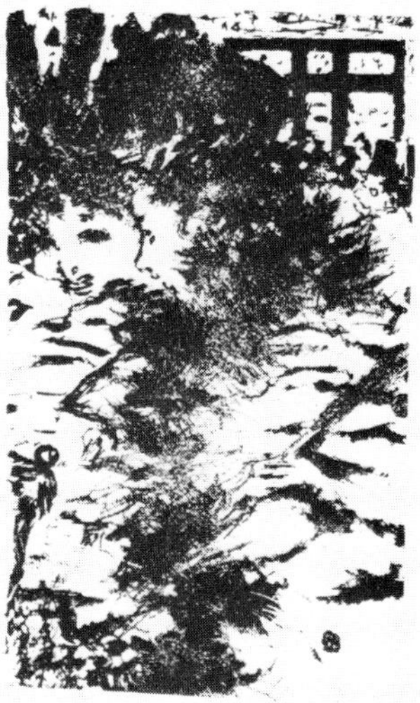
20

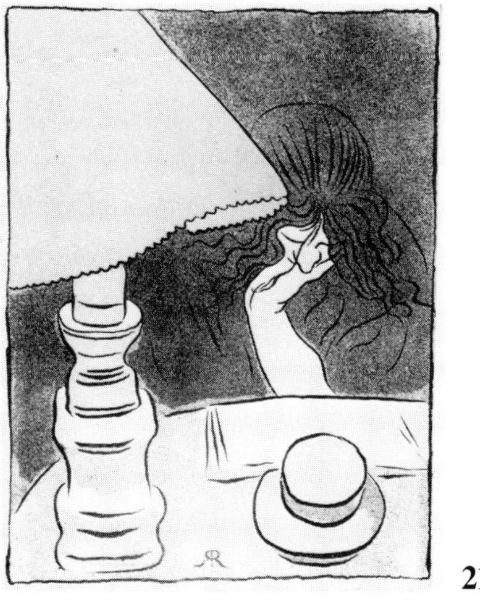
21

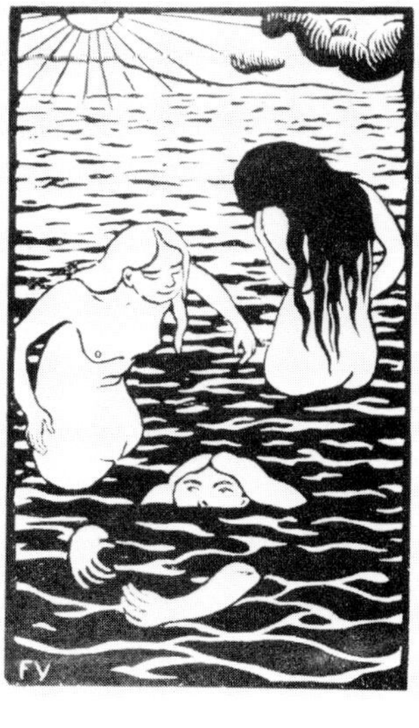
22

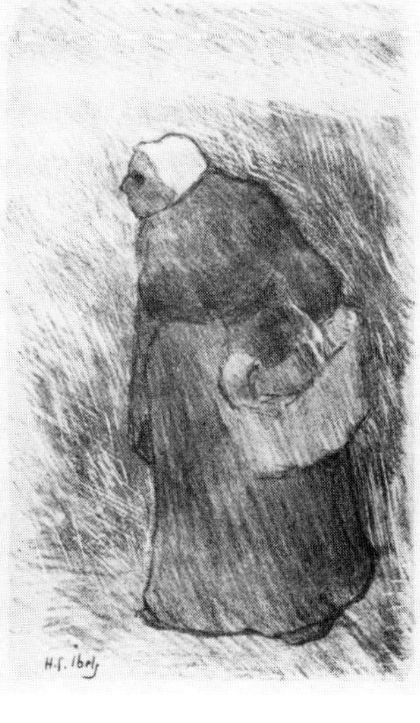
24

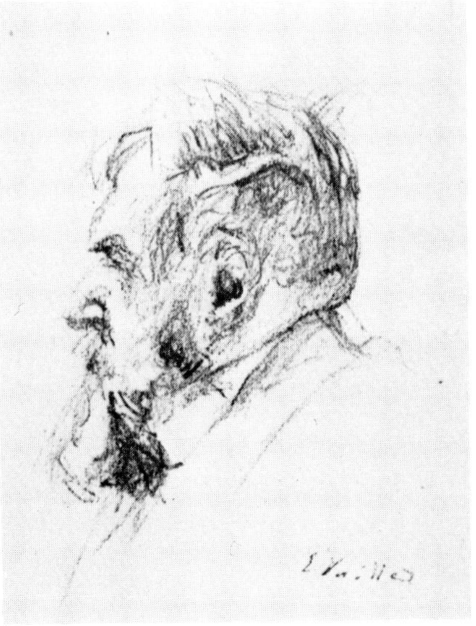

25

25.* Edouard Vuillard
Tristan Bernard, 1924
Lithograph printed in black
h. 12 x w. 9 cm.

Tristan Bernard was born in Besançon in 1866. He began his career as a business consultant and lawyer and started writing in 1891. As one-time editor of *La revue blanche,* he met Bonnard, Vuillard, and Toulouse-Lautrec. Bernard went on to become a distinguished author, journalist, and sportsman. As the latter, he became director of the Seine and Buffalo velodromes in 1895 and was responsible for introducing Toulouse-Lautrec to the world of cycling. Bernard died in Paris on December 7, 1947.

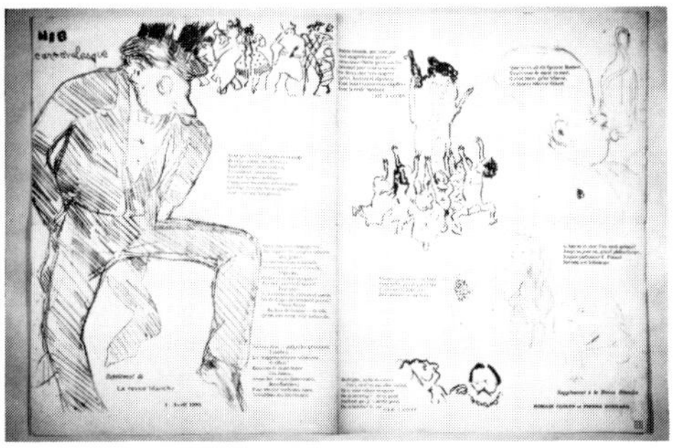

26

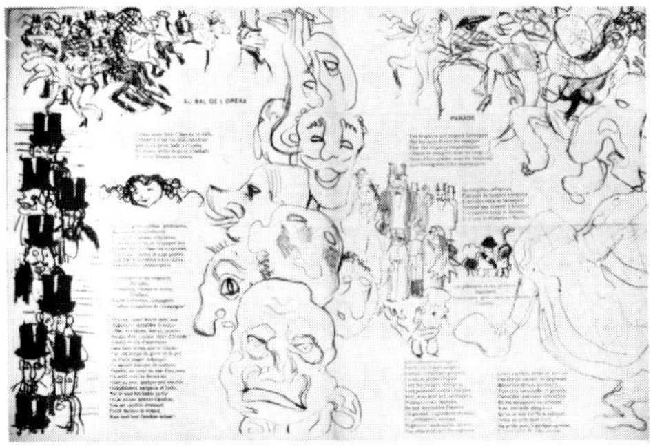

26A

26.* Pierre Bonnard
NIB/Carnavalesque
Insert for ***La revue blanche,*** 1895
Two-sided lithograph printed in black
h. 32.9 x w. 50 cm.

NIB (slang for "nothing") was edited by Toulouse-Lautrec and Tristan Bernard and appeared as a two-sided insert in *La revue blanche.* Only three issues were produced, and each represents complete collaboration between artist and writer: the issue for January 1895, between Toulouse-Lautrec and Bernard; February 1895, Vallotton and Jules Renard; and this example, April 1895, Bonnard and Romain Coolus.

27.** Pierre Bonnard
La revue blanche, 1894
Lithographic poster printed in four colors
h. 80 x w. 62 cm.

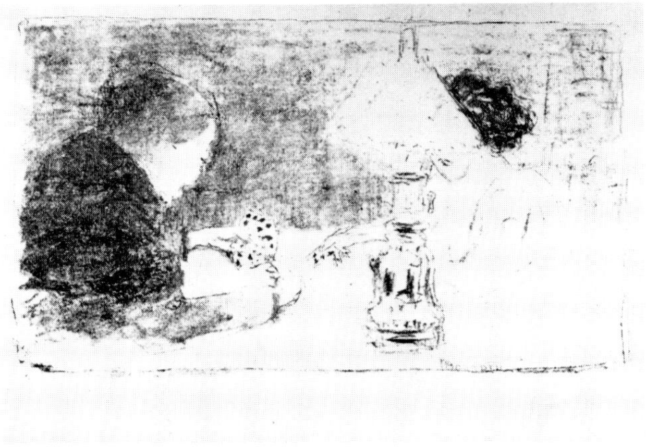

28

28.* Pierre Bonnard
La partie de cartes sous la lampe
Published by ***L'Epreuve,*** 1895
Deluxe, signed lithograph printed in dark blue-gray
h. 13.7 x w. 24 cm.

l'Epreuve was founded in December 1894 under the direction of the 24-year-old artist Maurice Dumont. The printing was done by Paul Lemaire at Dumont's studio. It was issued in 12 monthly portfolios of 10 prints each in editions of 215 (200 regular and 15 deluxe, signed issues) by artists working in various media. Although lithographs dominated the portfolios, color lithography was excluded, possibly because of limitations in the printing facilities. The five deluxe color lithography

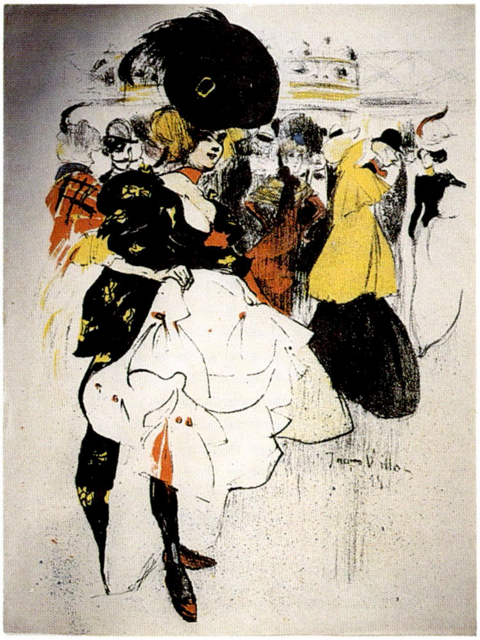

6

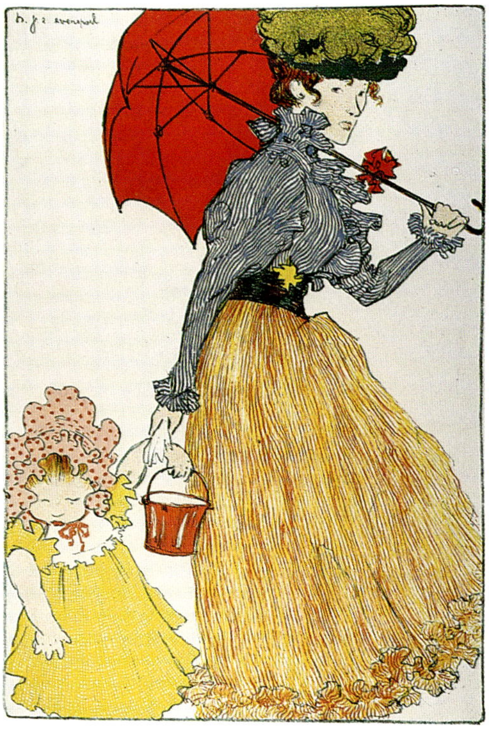

31

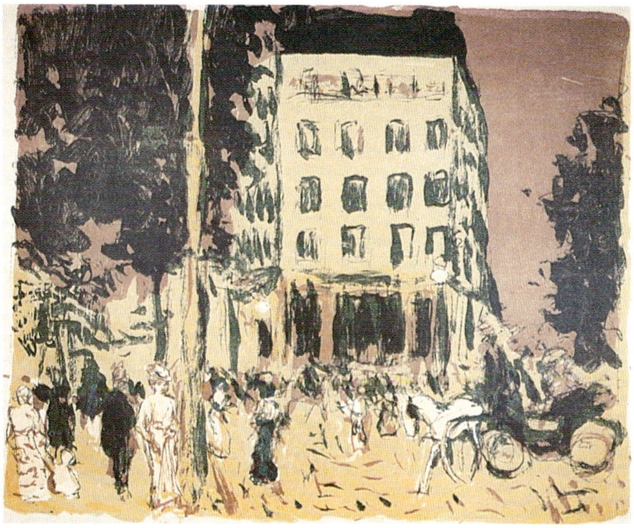

37

portfolios proposed for 1896 were never realized, and the publication ceased production after July 1895.

Dumont was responsible for inventing the process known as glyptotype: printing from a relief plate so that ink areas pressed deeply into the paper and unprinted areas of paper appeared in relief.

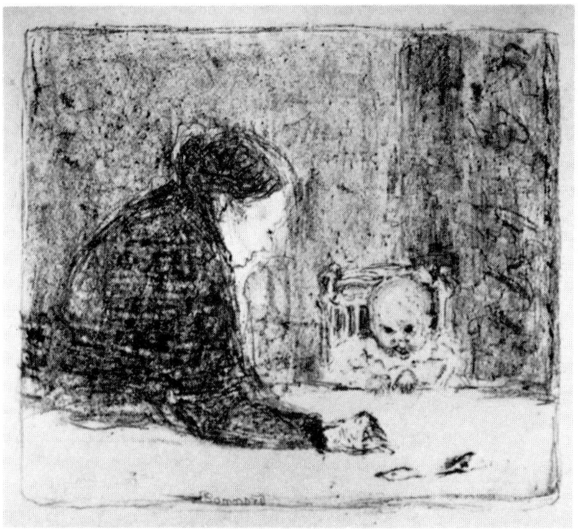

29

29.* Pierre Bonnard
The Great-Grandmother
Published by ***L'Epreuve,*** 1895
Lithograph printed in gray-green
h. 20 x w. 23 cm.

In this print, Bonnard's maternal grandmother, Madame Mertzdorff, is seen with his sister Andrée Terrasse's baby, probably Renée, born in December 1894. Andrée was married to the composer Claude Terrasse, for whom Bonnard illustrated numerous music books, song sheets including those for the *Répertoire des pantins* (figs. 61-63), and the music primer *Petit solfège illustré* (fig. 95) as well as *Petites scènes familières* represented here by the lithographic illustration for "La chanson du grand-père" (fig. 55).

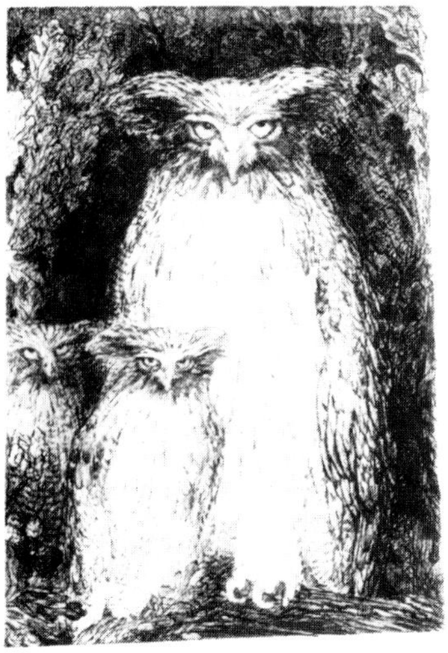

30

30.* Henry de Groux
Les grands ducs
Published by ***L'Epreuve,*** 1895
Pencil-signed lithograph printed in black
h. 34.5 x w. 25 cm.

Henry de Groux was born in Brussels, Belgium, in 1867. At a banquet given by the Société des XX on January 18, 1890, in Brussels, de Groux criticized the work of van Gogh, and Toulouse-Lautrec was so outraged at criticism of one whom he considered an artistic genius that he challenged de Groux to a duel. The members of the Société des XX were equally indignant at de Groux's discourteous behavior, and he was not only obliged to apologize but forced to resign from the group as well. De Groux died in Marseille in 1930.

The Société des XX, probably the most advanced avant-garde exhibition society in Europe, was founded in 1884 by James Ensor, Théo van Rysselberghe, and Fernald Khnopff with Octave Maus as secretary; they were soon joined by Jan Toorop, Rodin, Signac, van de Velde, and Georges Mine. The group was widely influenced: in England, from Whistler to the pre-Raphaelites; in France, impressionism, symbolism, and neoimpressionism. They were also among the principal exponents of art nouveau. The Société des XX was supported by the review *L'Art moderne*. In 1894 it was reorganized as La Libre Esthétique.

31.** Henri-Jacques Evenepoel
Au square
Published in ***L'Estampe moderne,*** 1897
Lithograph printed in five colors
h. 33 x w. 23 cm.

L'Estampe moderne was published from May 1897 until April 1899 by Charles Masson and H. Piazza and printed by Champenois. It catered to a larger, less sophisticated clientele than its predecessor *L'Estampe originale* and consisted of 24 monthly portfolios of four "original prints," the majority being color lithographs in editions of 150. Although printed on cheaper papers and more illustrative than its predecessors, its main weakness was in its use of

32 collotypes or photolithographs after drawings. Its saving graces are the color lithographs by Alphonse Mucha, Louis John Rhead, Georges Munier, Dillon, de Feure, and this Evenepohl. These prints maintained the artistic standards of Marty and Vollard, yet are the exceptions not the rule.

Evenepoel was a Belgian artist who was born in 1872 and died in 1899.

32.** Victor Mignot
Père Noël
Frontispiece for ***Album de contes Noël,*** c. 1895
Lithograph printed in six colors
h. 39.5 x w. 27.5 cm.

Victor Mignot, a Belgian artist, was born in 1872 and died in 1916.

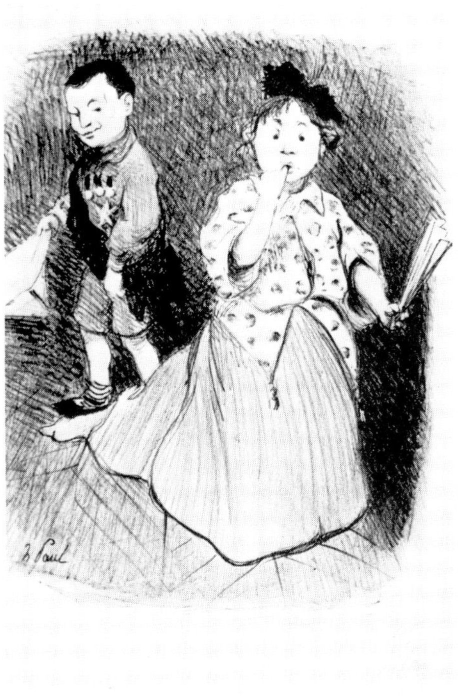

33

33.* Hermann-René-Georges Paul (Hermann-Paul)
Untitled, c. 1895
Lithograph printed in black
h. 27 x w. 22 cm.

Hermann-René-Georges Paul, known as Hermann-Paul, was born in Paris in 1864, son of Constantin Paul, a doctor. He attended the Académie Julian, became an ardent print maker and illustrator, and created covers and illustrations for *L'Escarmouche* as well as other journals. Hermann-Paul's style and use of caricature were similar to and have often been compared to that of Toulouse-Lautrec. He died in 1940.

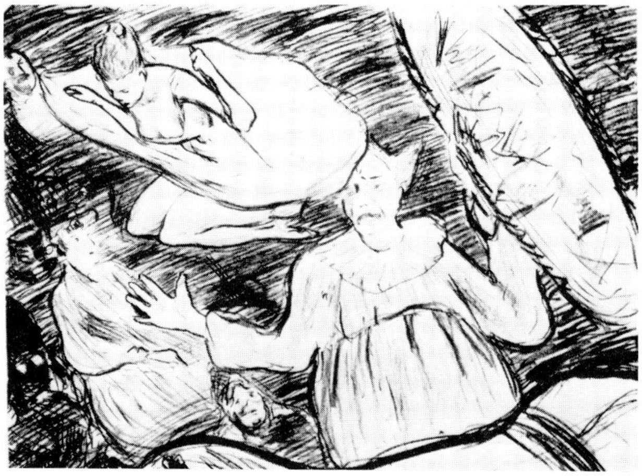

34

34.* Henri-Gabriel Ibels
Bird's-Eye View of the Circus
Published for ***Les demi-cabots,*** 1895
Signed lithograph printed in black
h. 21.6 x w. 29.7 cm.

In 1895 Ibels did a portfolio of 14 etchings titled *Les forains* featuring circus subjects. This lithograph, originally intended for *Les forains,* was later used to illustrate a poem about gymnasts by his brother André Ibels for *Les demi-cabots.* In his circus and theater works, Ibels shared a common thematic interest with Toulouse-Lautrec.

35.** Henri-Edmund Cross
Champs-Elysée, 1898
Lithograph printed in five colors
h. 12.5 x w. 26 cm.

Born Henri-Edmund Delacroix May 20, 1856, in Douai, France, he later anglicized his name to Cross. He began his studies at the Lille Académie des Beaux-Arts and moved to Paris in 1876. Cross exhibited at the Salon in 1881 and at the Salon des Indépendants in 1884, having by this time come in contact with the neoimpressionists Seurat and Signac. This connection was responsible for his producing this pointillist print. According to Seurat and Signac, pointillism was the scientific and logical development of impressionism. They, along with Cross, practiced the optical blending of color, their choice of coloring being based on Chevreul's "Chromatic Circle" of exact corresponding color complements.

In 1894 Meier Graefe and Otto Julius Bierbaum of Berlin founded the German periodical *Pan,* an artistic and literary review, in which Cross's *Champs-Elysée* was published in 1898.

Cross died May 16, 1910, at Saint-Clair near Le Lavendon, France.

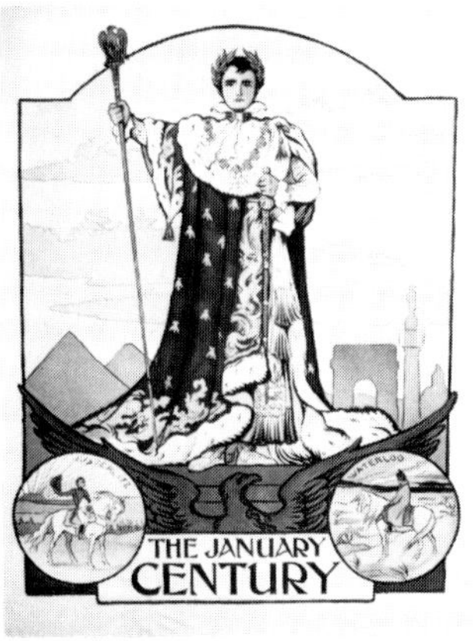

36

36.* Lucien Marie Françoise Métivet
Napoléon
Poster for ***Century Magazine,*** January 1895
Lithograph printed in six colors
h. 57 x w. 46 cm.

This poster was designed for a competition sponsored by Boussod, Valadon et Cie., publishers of *Le Figaro illustré.* Eighteen artists including Toulouse-Lautrec designed pieces for the competition, and it was assumed that Toulouse-Lautrec's entry would win. Finalists included Chartier, Dupray, and this competition-winning Métivet. The more avant-garde representations were refused by the traditional Salon-oriented judges, Edouard Detaille, Léon Gérome, and Georges Vibert.

Lucien Marie Françoise Métivet was born in Paris in 1863. He later became friends with Toulouse-Lautrec at Cormon's studio after having left the Académie Julian. He is primarily remembered not for his paintings and prints, but for his costume designs and caricature illustrations for books and publications, in particular *Le Rire* (fig. 76; no. 77). He created numerous costume designs and book illustrations for author/playwright Catulle Mendès. Métivet died in 1937.

37.** Pierre Bonnard
Les boulevards
Published in ***Das Mappenwerk der Insel,*** 1900
Lithograph printed in four colors
h. 27 x w. 33.4 cm.

Les boulevards was included in an album of 24 lithographs published by the German periodical *Das Mappenwerk der Insel,* Leipzig, Germany, in 1900. Also included in the album was Vuillard's *Une galerie au gymnase* (pl. 38).

38.** Edouard Vuillard
Une galerie au gymnase
Published in ***Das Mappenwerk der Insel,*** 1900
Lithograph printed in five colors
h. 25 x w. 19.5 cm.

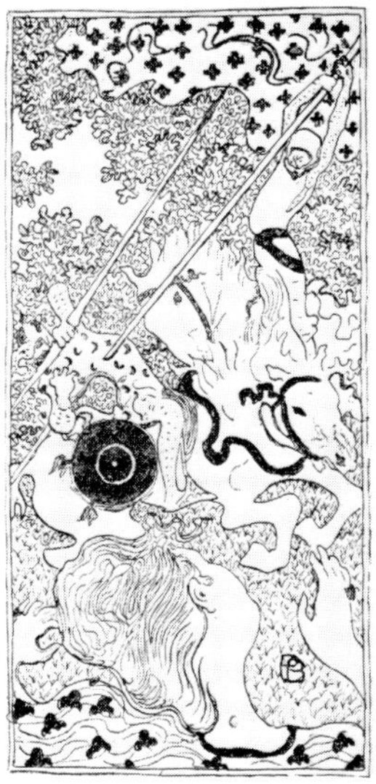

39

39.* Pierre Bonnard
Le geste du roy
Program for Théâtre d'Art, 1891-92 season
Photomechanical print in black
h. 14.2 x w. 6.9 cm.

Le geste du roy served as the cover illustration for the program of the premier 1891-92 season of Paul Fort's symbolist Théâtre d'Art. The theater rapidly attracted Lugné-Poe and the support of the Nabis—all of whom were moving away from the dying popularity of the realist dramas presented by Antoine's Théâtre Libre. The theater was backed by Malarmé, Verlaine, Verhaeren, and Maeterlinck with Sérusier and Gauguin as designers. Bonnard, Vuillard, and Ibels were later additions to the design group.

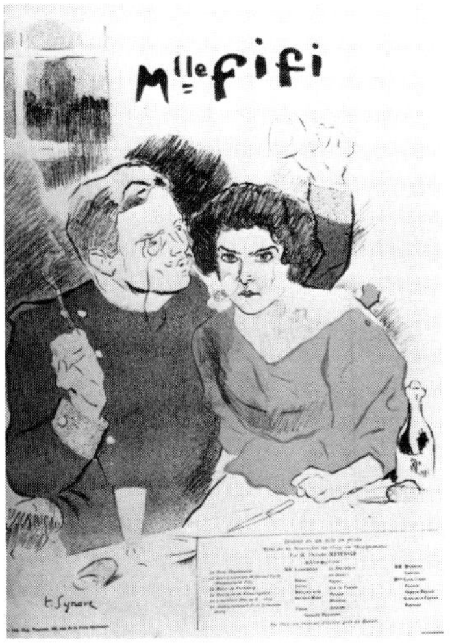

40

40.* Tancrède Synave
Mlle. Fifi
Program for Théâtre Libre, 1895-96 season
Lithograph printed in five colors
h. 30.8 x w. 23.3 cm.

This program cover was for *Mlle. Fifi,* the third spectacle of the Théâtre Libre's 1895-96 season.

The Théâtre Libre was founded in March 1887 by actor/producer André Antoine, who introduced realism to the French stage with works by Ibsen, Strindberg, Zola, and others. It was here that Lugné-Poe began his acting career in 1888. This experimental theater used the talents of radical young artists to illustrate its program covers. During the nine years that the theater existed, 35 black-and-white or color programs were produced. By 1893 realism in the theater had run its course and was losing its audience and artistic relevance as symbolism began to emerge. Antoine sold the theater in 1895.

Synave was born in Paris in 1860.

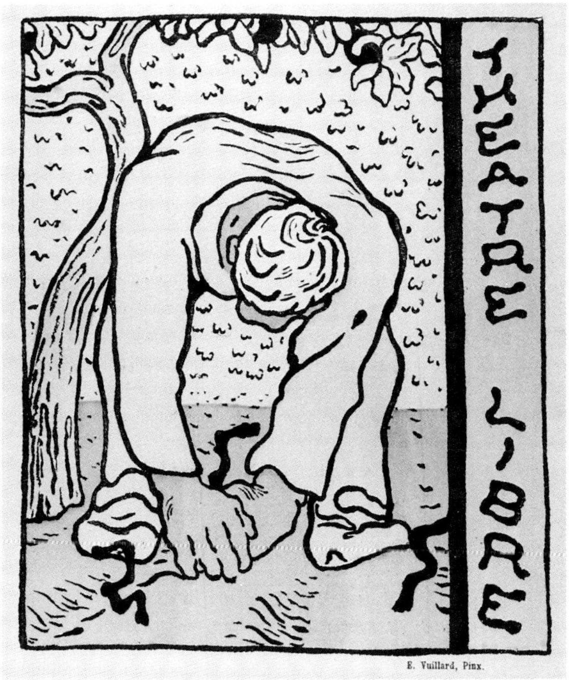

41

41.* Edouard Vuillard
Monsieur Bute
Program for Théâtre Libre, 1890
Photorelief print with four-color stencil
h. 19.5 x w. 16.5 cm.

This was Vuillard's first published theater program design. Although strongly influenced by the peasants of van Gogh, it is marked by Vuillard's urban rather than van Gogh's suburban sensibility.

42. Jehan-Georges Vibert
Le cuivre
Program for Théâtre Libre, 1895-96 season
Lithograph printed in black on rose paper
h. 23 x w. 31 cm.

Jehan-Georges Vibert was born in Paris in 1840 and died there in 1902. Like many of his contemporaries, he had early ambitions to be a history painter. He studied at the École des Beaux-Arts and in the ateliers of Felix Picot and Barrias and began exhibiting in the Salon in 1863. During the 1870s he wrote several comedies that were produced. In 1880 he was among the founding members of the Society of French Watercolorists. He collected Japanese art, and his Paris residence became a meeting place for a group of younger artists called the Cercle de St. Arnaud. A watercolor by Vibert, *A Cardinal,* 1902, can be seen in the Taft Museum collection.

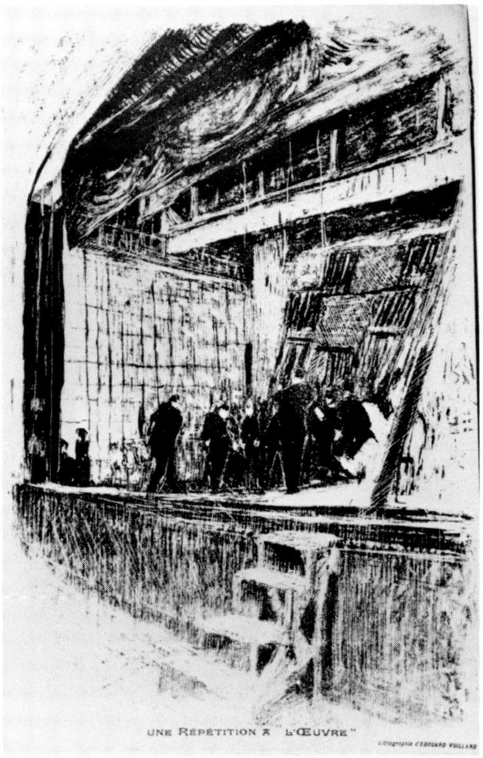

43

43.* Edouard Vuillard
Répétition à l'Oeuvre, 1903
Lithograph printed in black
h. 20.5 x w. 30 cm.

The Théâtre de l'Oeuvre was founded in May 1893 by Aurélien-Marie Lugné-Poe who had previously been associated with Antoine's Théâtre Libre and Paul Fort's Théâtre d'Art. Prior to studying at the

Conservatoire de Musique et de la Declamation, while still a student at the Lycée Condorcet, he met Bonnard, Vuillard, and Denis; they shared living quarters at 28 rue Pigalle. Vuillard proposed the name *"oeuvre"* meaning "work." Lugné-Poe's primary interest was in having the "work" stand on its own right. The Théâtre de l'Oeuvre specialized in Scandinavian and "idealistic" productions and symbolist drama.

Lugné-Poe continued the practice of commissioning young artists to create program designs as well as sets and costumes. Most of the designs were executed by members of the Nabis group. Lugné-Poe shared the symbolist sympathies of the Nabis and was an indefatigable supporter of their art. This was Vuillard's last theater program.

44.* Edouard Vuillard
Rosmersholm
Program for Théâtre de l'Oeuvre, 1893
Lithograph printed in black
h. 21 x w. 31.5 cm.

Lugné-Poe chose Henrik Ibsen's *Rosmersholm* for the opening production of the Théâtre de l'Oeuvre, October 6, 1893. The sets for the production were designed by Bonnard and Sérusier.

45.* Edouard Vuillard
Un ennemi du peuple
Program for Théâtre de l'Oeuvre, 1893
Lithograph printed in black
h. 22 x w. 30.5 cm.

Henrik Ibsen's *An Enemy of the People,* a play about water pollution, opened at the Théâtre de l'Oeuvre on November 8, 1893.

46.* Henri de Toulouse-Lautrec
Le chariot de terre cuite
Program for Théâtre de l'Oeuvre, 1895
Lithograph printed in blue on rose-tinted ground
h. 43.5 x w. 28 cm.

Victor Barrucand's five-act, French adaptation of the classical Hindu drama *The Terra-Cotta Chariot* opened at the Théâtre de l'Oeuvre, January 22, 1895. The sets for the production were designed by Louis Valtat and Toulouse-Lautrec, his only executed set design. This program shows half of the first-act set, a faithful model of the wooden elephant from the garden of the Moulin Rouge, with Toulouse-Lautrec's anarchist friend Félix Fénéon atop delivering the prologue. Toulouse-Lautrec also designed the book

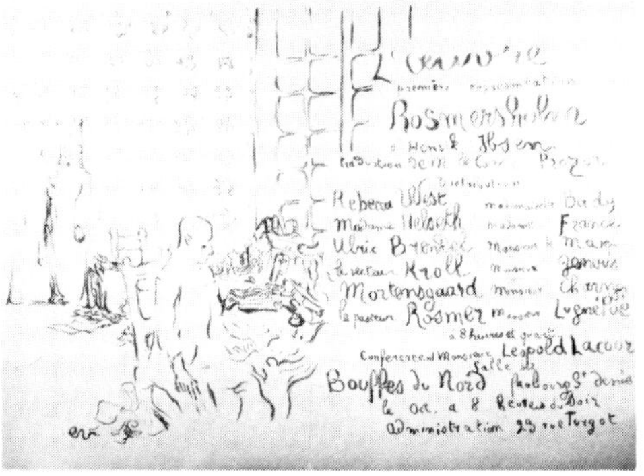

44

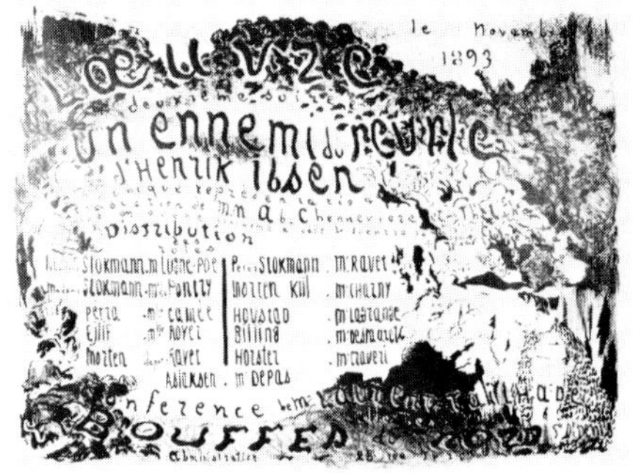

45

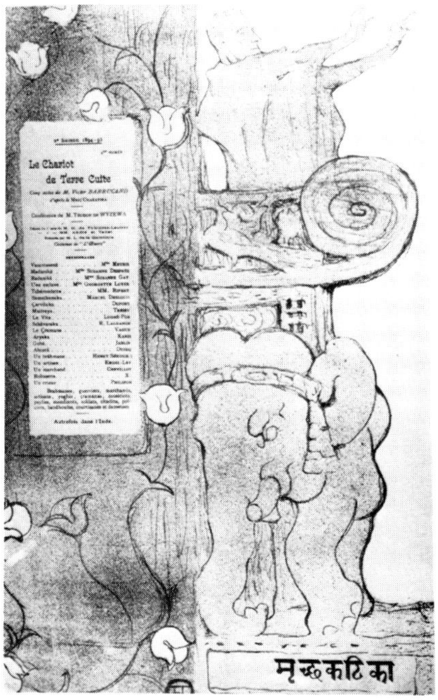

46

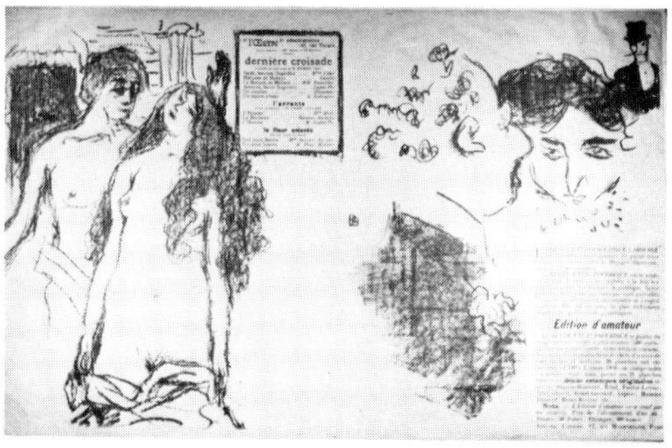

47

cover for Barrucand's adaptation published by Albert Savine in 1895.

47.* Pierre Bonnard
Dernière croisade
Program for Théâtre de l'Oeuvre, 1896
Lithograph printed in gray
h. 30 x w. 49.5 cm.

The Théâtre de l'Oeuvre on April 24, 1896, presented the play *Dernière croisade* by Maxime Gray. In the play, Baron Gugenfeld is converting to Catholicism for his wife while she uses the time he spends studying religion to practice her infidelity with the Marquis de Maltaux. The front of the cover depicts the Marquis in top hat observing the Baron and Baroness from afar. The nudes on the back cover represent one of the other plays in the trilogy featured on this bill, which also included *L'Errant* by Pierre Quillard and Jules Arene's translation of the Chinese play *La fleur enlevée.*

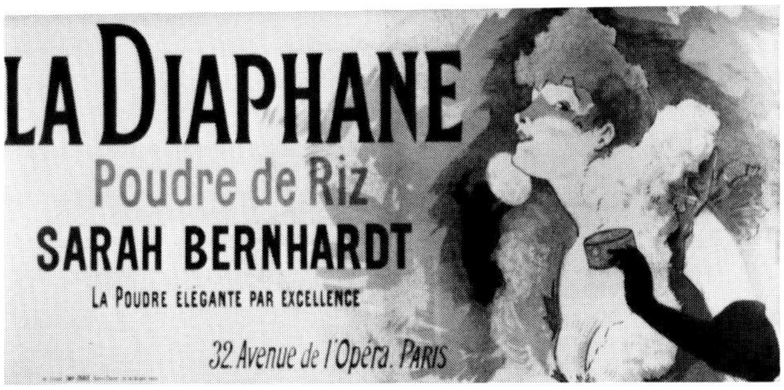

48

48.* Jules Chéret
La Diaphane, 1890
Lithographic poster printed in five colors
h. 40 x w. 84 cm.

Born in 1836, Jules Chéret was apprenticed to a commercial lithographer by 1849. Shortly after this, he moved to the lithographic shop of Bouasse-Lebel, which specialized in religious materials. During his time there Chéret frequented the Louvre where he was so inspired by Antoine Watteau, the 18th-century French colorist, that he began studies with Lecoque de Boisbaudran at the École Nationale de Dessin.

By 1855 Chéret had produced three black-and-white posters. He received his first color poster commission for Jacques Offenbach's operetta *Orphée aux enfers* in 1858. Because of a lack of additional commissions Chéret relocated in London to design for the Rimmel Perfume manufacturers. In 1866 Rimmel backed Chéret's return to Paris and the establishment of his first print shop specializing in posters. Through this backing Chéret was able to found an art form, a commercial marketing approach, and a thriving lithographic industry almost singlehandedly—simplifying the techniques for the medium and making the process accessible to nearly everyone. In 1869, the shop moved to the rue Brunel and in 1890 to 20 rue Bergère, merging with Alban Chaix who had assumed the business end of Chéret's printing house in 1881.

Chéret's posters combine the 18th-century French rococo grace, femininity, and coloration of Watteau and Greuze with the traditional European mural composition of Tiepolo. Until 1894 the lettering was executed by Madaré. The posters communicated simply, directly, and decoratively.

Charlotte Wiehe, the Danish actress and dancer, was Chéret's favorite model. Through her he created the epitome of the girl of the 1880s and 1890s, the "Chérette," who was to signify the self-indulgent, superficial pleasures, the spirit of the *fin de siècle.*

Until 1890 Chéret remained the leading poster artist of Paris. From 1866 through the 1890s he produced over 1000 posters, book covers, menus, song sheets, etc. He began publishing *Les maîtres de l'affiche* with Chaix in 1896.

Chéret died in Nice in 1932.

In this poster the famous French actress Sarah Bernhardt endorses La Diaphane rice facial powder.

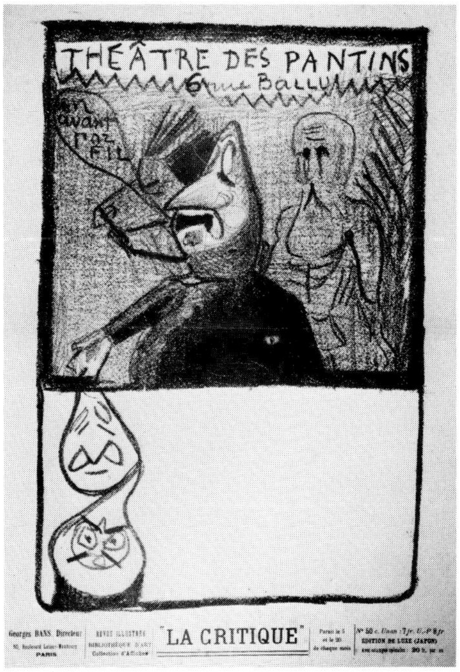

49

49.* Alfred Jarry
Répertoire des pantins
Program cover for ***Ubu Roi,*** before lettering, 1898
Lithograph printed in dark green
h. 31.7 x w. 22.7 cm.

This program cover was designed by Alfred Jarry for his "Ubu" series at the Théâtre des Pantins, the first production of which was *Ubu Roi,* January 20, 1898. The actual theatrical debut of *Ubu Roi* was at the Théâtre de l'Oeuvre on December 10, 1896. Jarry also designed the sheet music for all other productions at the Théâtre des Pantins, some of which are included in this exhibition (figs. 61-63).

A writer and playwright, Jarry became associated with Bonnard and Vuillard through *La revue blanche,* to which he contributed regularly from 1896 to 1903, and the Théâtre de l'Oeuvre and Lugné-Poe.

50.** Henri Rivière
Théâtre du chat noir, c. 1887
Photomechanical poster stenciled in pale blue-green
h. 53.5 x w. 39.5 cm.

The cabaret Le Chat Noir opened in January 1881 under the direction of Rodolphe Salis. The Chat Noir immediately attracted a large following of artists, writers, and musicians. Many of the poets and *chansonniers* were formerly members of the Hydropathes and included their former leader Émile Goudeau as well as Mac Nab, Anatole France, Rollinat, Marcel Legay, and Catulle Mendès and later Jehan Rictus, Mallarmé, Paul Verlaine, Maupassant, and others. The artists included George Auriol, Adolphe Willette, Steinlen, Toulouse-Lautrec, Forain, and Rivière. Musicians and performers included Jean Richepin, Georges Fagerolle, Albert Tinchant, Charles de Sivery, Claude Debussy, Delmet, Yvette Guilbert, Théréza, Coquelin, and Sarah Bernhardt. Goudeau established the Friday and Saturday "literary soirées" and the Wednesday *"absinthes littéraries."* A usual evening consisted of recitations by poets and writers and recitals by musicians, composers, and singers with Salis introducing the program of activities.

On June 10, 1885, the Chat Noir moved to new quarters on the rue de Laval (rue Victor Masse). Here, Salis proposed a new attraction to Parisian cabaret goers, the shadow theater. Performances were held on the second floor of the new location in the Salle des Fêtes. The "plays" of the "new" Théâtre d'Ombres were often historical in nature, yet many were mystical and religious dramas or comedies. From 1887 to 1896 some 43 plays were produced by 19 different artists including Henri Rivière (1864-1951), who operated the theater. Henri Somm's "L'Éléphant" was the premier production and opened all performances during the shadow theater's existence. The ingenious use of light play and shadows, scenes painted on transparent or translucent papers or superimposed on colored glass panels, zinc cutouts, and Japanese-style puppets created unparalleled cinematographic effects on the screen of the shadow theater stage. The plays were then underscored by musical and choral accompaniment and narration.

The various artists of the Chat Noir identified with the immediate Montmartre environment and through their artistic endeavors raised the local popular culture into an art that strongly influenced the literary mainstream. The Chat Noir offered an amazingly rich cross section of the arts and entertainment and had no equal. It closed its doors in 1897, a few months prior to the death of Salis.

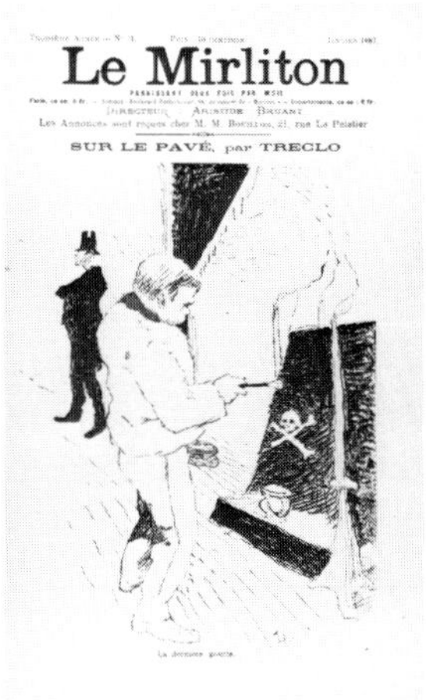

51

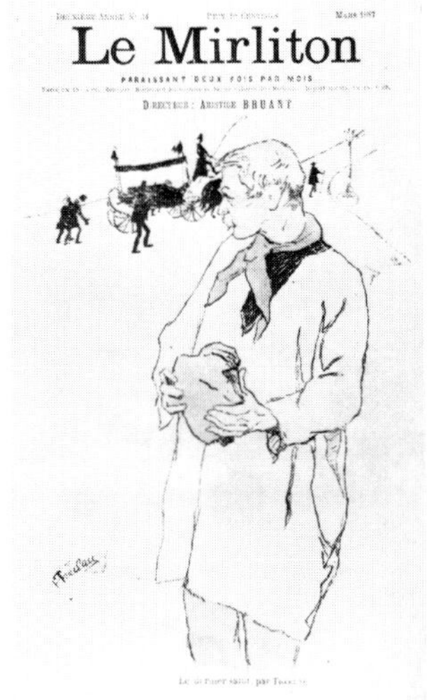

52

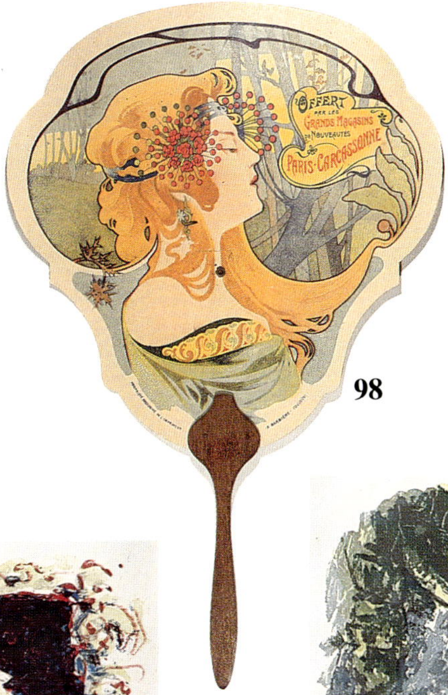

OFFERT
PAR LES
GRANDS MAGASINS
DE NOUVEAUTES
PARIS-CARCASSONNE

98

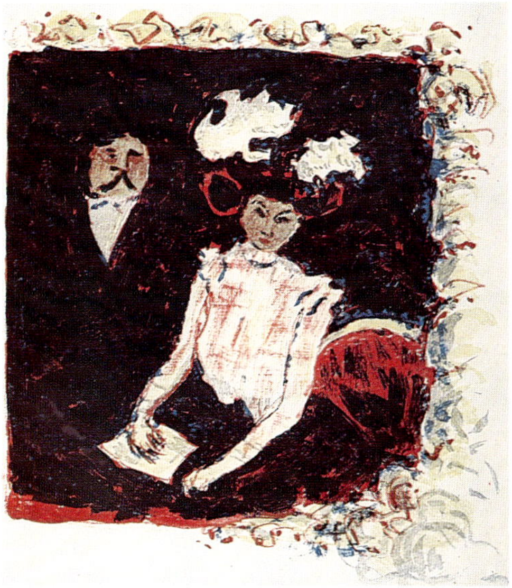

3

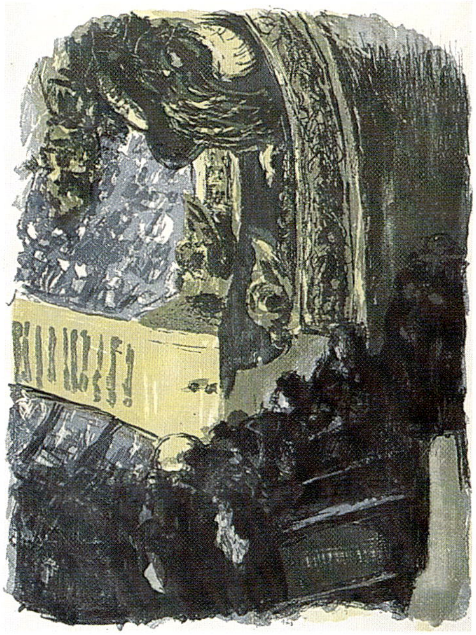

38

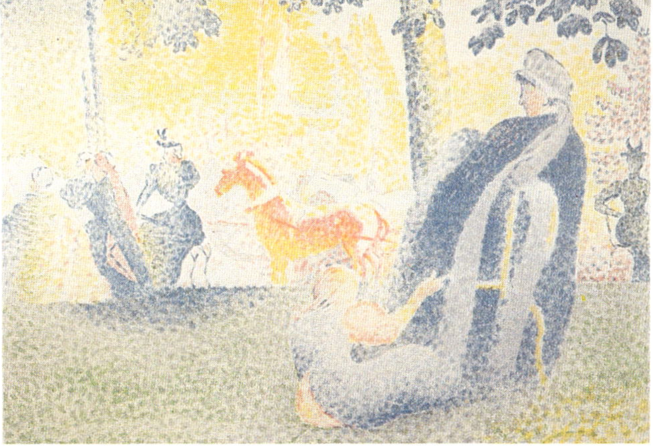

35

51.* Henri de Toulouse-Lautrec
La dernière goutte
Cover for ***Le Mirliton,*** January 1887
Photomechanical print stenciled in red
h. 27.8 x w. 17.6 cm.

The publication *Le Mirliton* began production in the fall of 1885 under the direction of Aristide Bruant for his cabaret of the same name. *Le Mirliton* was published sporadically and was primarily used to disseminate Bruant's songs. Throughout its 10-year existence the photorelief covers were stencil colored by hand. Although Steinlen was *Le Mirliton's* principal illustrator, it was in these cover illustrations that Toulouse-Lautrec first used color (fig. 52). The covers were signed with his anagram "Tréclau," used as a result of family disagreement with his new lifestyle and its possible discredit to the family name. This is the primary reason the Toulouse portion of his name remained merely a "T" in both signature and monogram throughout his life.

52.* Henri de Toulouse-Lautrec
Le dernier salut
Cover for ***Le Mirliton,*** March 1887
Photomechanical print stenciled in four colors
h. 27.8 x w. 17.6 cm.

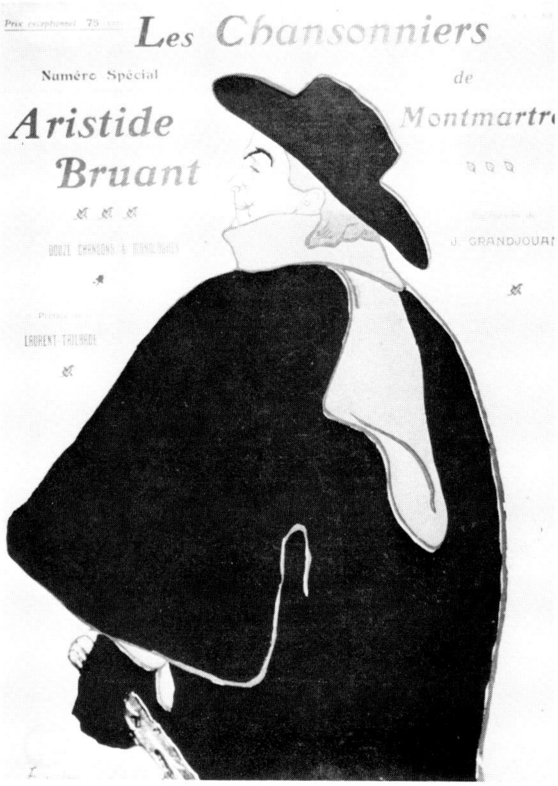

53

53.* Henri de Toulouse-Lautrec
Les chansonniers de Montmartre: Aristide Bruant
Sheet music cover, 1906
Lithograph printed in three colors
h. 36 x w. 27.5 cm.

This sheet music cover design for *Les chansonniers de Montmartre: Aristide Bruant* was adapted from the 1893 poster *Aristide Bruant dans son cabaret* by Toulouse-Lautrec. The song book contains 12 of Bruant's original songs or collaborations.

Aristide Bruant was born in Courtenay in 1851 and moved to Paris at age 15 with his poor parents. By 1875, following his enlistment in the French army during the Franco-Prussian War, Bruant became interested in the problems of the people inhabiting the poorer districts of Paris. He began to write verses and monologues dealing with these topics, realistic songs akin to Zola's novels. Originally he set his verses to popular tunes but later began composing his own original music.

Following numerous successful engagements at a variety of *cafés-concerts,* Bruant began performing regularly at the Chat Noir, establishing his reputation. In June 1885, when the Chat Noir moved to a larger establishment, Bruant took over the old premises and opened Le Mirliton. Coinciding with the opening was the arrival of Toulouse-Lautrec in Montmartre, and they became immediate friends. Bruant's songs and Toulouse-Lautrec's art drew from the same subject matter and contained the same universal qualities—the same living reality that is altogether independent of time and place.

Bruant continued to perform and write throughout his life. He died February 11, 1925, at Courtenay, France.

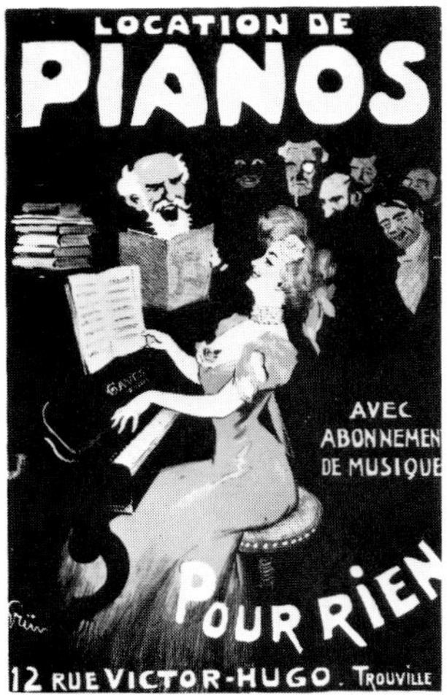

54

54.* Jules-Alexandre Grün
Location de pianos pour rien, c. 1895
Lithographic poster printed in three colors
h. 55 x w. 37.5 cm.

Jules-Alexandre Grün was born May 26, 1868. He began his education at the Commercial College but soon left to enter the studio of opera-set painter Lavastre where he specifically learned to draw and, as a result, had his first painting accepted at the Salon in 1886. He later studied at the Guillemet Studio and continued to exhibit at the Salon.

Grün began designing posters in 1891 for the *cafés-concerts* and theaters, which were the subject of the majority of his poster works. Through the songwriter Xanrof, he began illustrating music books and sheet music. His style was strongly influenced by Vallotton: a bold use of black and white, negative and positive, with red often the second and only color. He was most famous for his sultry-to-frolicsome depictions of Parisian police. Grün died February 15, 1934.

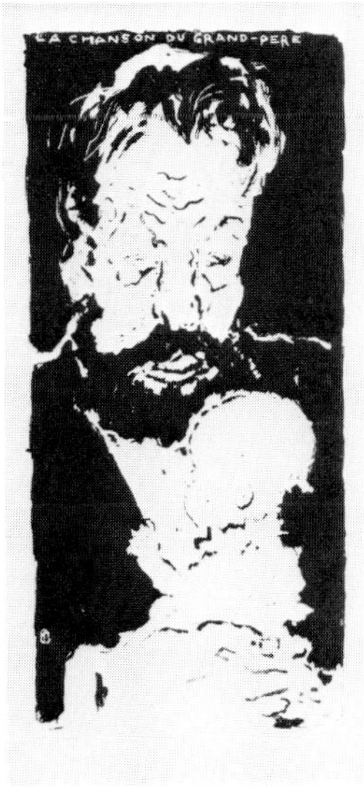

55

55.* Pierre Bonnard
La chanson du grand-père
Proof from ***Petites scènes familières,*** 1893
Lithographic proof printed in black
h. 22.5 x w. 10.5 cm.

La chanson du grand-père was one of 20 illustrations for the music book *Petites scènes familières* by Claude Terrasse, Bonnard's brother-in-law. The series included the cover and illustrations for 19 songs.

56. René Péan
Pianos A. Bord, c. 1890
Lithographic poster printed in six colors
h. 77 x w. 57 cm.

57.** Maurice Denis
Concerts du petit frère et de la petite soeur
Sheet music design for André Rossignol, 1903
Lithograph printed in three colors
h. 34.5 x w. 27 cm.

Maurice Denis was born November 25, 1870, in Granville. He began his studies at the Pension Villon and the Lycée Condorcet and in 1888 entered the Académie Julian. In 1889 he became an original member of the Nabis and was known as the "Nabis of beautiful icons." As an extremely able writer, he became the spokesman for the Nabis, writing under the pseudonym Pierre Louis. After the turn of the century, Denis's art took on a distinctly religious air. He died November 3, 1943, in a car accident in Paris.

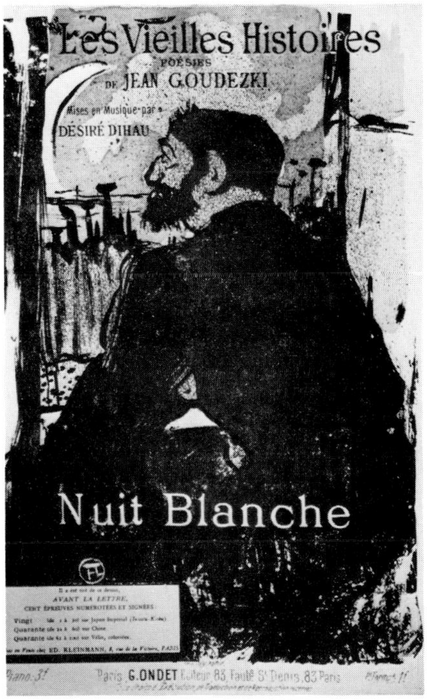

58

58.* Henri de Toulouse-Lautrec
Nuit blanche
Song sheet for ***Les vielles histoires,*** 1893
Lithograph stenciled in two colors
h. 25.2 x w. 17.5 cm.

Nuit blanche and *Sagesse* (pl. 59), illustrated song sheets, were produced for Désiré Dihau who composed the music for five romantic poems titled *Les vielles histoires* by singer/poet Jean Goudeżki. Additional pieces were illustrated by Ibels and Henri Rachou. The illustrations were commissioned in 1893 by the music publisher Ondet at the insistence of Ibels who was interested in having artists involved in this field. Ondet was considered a publisher of art as well, in that he usually produced editions of 100 prints without lettering in conjunction with the song sheets. The designs were often hand colored by stenciling.

The Dihaus were a family of musicians from Lille and distant cousins of Toulouse-Lautrec. Désiré had earlier won first prize at the Conservatoire and as a bassoonist performed with the Pasdeloup and Colonne ensembles and the Orchestre de l'Opéra. Désiré's sister, Marie, was a successful singer during the 1860s and 1870s, later taught voice and piano, and also played with the Orchestre de l'Opéra.

59.** Henri de Toulouse-Lautrec
Sagesse
Song sheet for ***Les vielles histoires,*** 1893
Lithograph stenciled in three colors
h. 26 x w. 18 cm.

60.** Henri de Toulouse-Lautrec
Carnot malade
Monologue sheet for ***Chansons du chat noir,*** 1893
Lithograph stenciled in four colors
h. 27.6 x w. 17.6 cm.

This satirical monologue concerns a liver attack suffered by Sadi Carnot, president of the Third Republic in 1893, and his subsequent treatment at Marly. Although the Third Republic was well established, its failure to accomplish significant social reforms led to an outbreak of anarchist activity, the climax of which was Carnot's assassination by Caserio in June 1894 at Lyon.

61.* Pierre Bonnard
La complainte de M. Benoît
Sheet music for ***Répertoire des pantins,*** 1898
Lithograph printed in black
h. 35 x w. 27 cm.

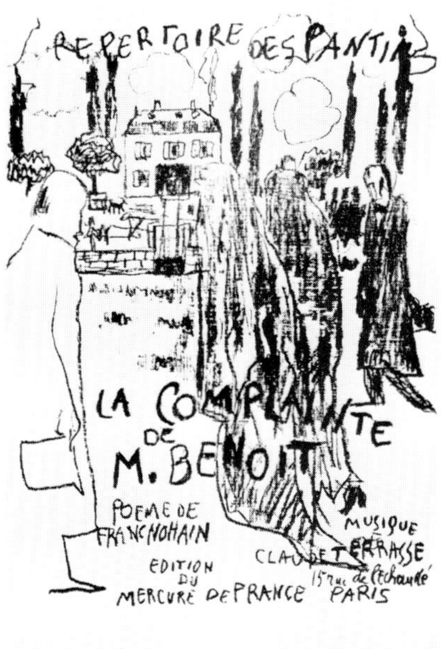

61

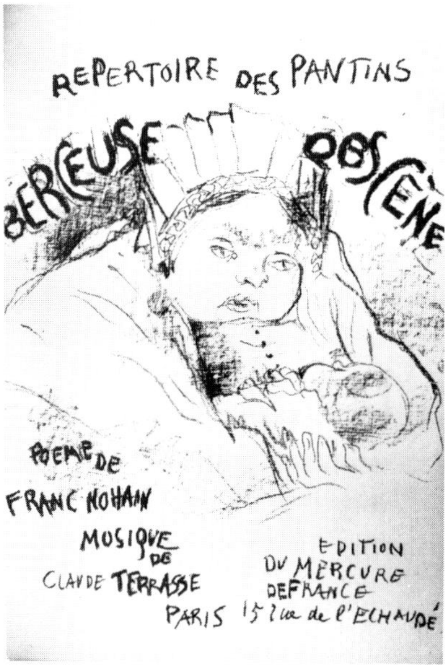

62

63

The Théâtre des Pantins, founded by Alfred Jarry, Franc Nohain, and Claude Terrasse, existed only a few years. The small marionette theater was located at the back of a courtyard on the first floor of Terrasse's living quarters. The motto of the theater was *"en avant par fil"* ("forward in single file"—*fil* meaning "file" or "string").

The interior decoration for the theater was designed by Vuillard in brilliant colors and by Bonnard with deftly executed silhouettes in black and gray. Terrasse composed the music for the performances to Nohain's often risqué lyrics. The sheet music designs were by Bonnard (figs. 62, 63), except for those for the "Ubu" series productions, which were designed by Jarry. The sheet music was published by the Mercure de France. Bonnard worked with Jarry, Terrasse, and Nohain in creating the wooden marionettes while Vuillard, Vallotton, and Bonnard created the sets and decorations.

62.* Pierre Bonnard
Berceuse Obscène
Sheet music for ***Répertoire des pantins,*** 1898
Lithograph printed in black
h. 35 x w. 27 cm.

63.* Pierre Bonnard
Paysage de neige
Sheet music for ***Répertoire des pantins,*** 1898
Lithograph printed in black
h. 35.2 x w. 27 cm.

64.** Jules-Alexandre Grün
Concert européen, 1900
Lithographic poster printed in five colors
h. 118 x w. 82 cm.

65.* Henri de Toulouse-Lautrec
Caudieux: Petit Casino
Published in ***Le café-concert,*** 1893
Lithograph printed in black
h. 27.5 x w. 21.8 cm.

In 1893 André Marty of *L'Estampe originale* commissioned Toulouse-Lautrec and Ibels to produce a portfolio of 22 lithographs based on popular *café-concert* performers appearing at Le Petit Casino, Les Ambassadeurs, and La Scala (figs. 66-69). The album was preceded by a 13-page text by Georges Montorgueil, chosen because as a writer his specialty was defending the cause of the performers in the concert halls. Ibels's two-color cover for the album featured the seated figure of Francisque Sarcey, drama critic for *Le Temps. Le café-concert* album originally sold for 20 francs.

Toulouse-Lautrec and Ibels were closely associated prior to this project. It was at Ibels's urging that Toulouse-Lautrec began lithography. Toulouse-Lautrec was also godfather to Ibels's son.

66.* Henri de Toulouse-Lautrec
Chanteur américain
Published in ***Le café-concert,*** 1893
Lithograph printed in black
h. 27.8 x w. 20.5 cm.

67.* Henri-Gabriel Ibels
Untitled
Published in ***Le café-concert,*** 1893
Lithograph printed in black
h. 28.5 x w. 21 cm.

68.* Henri-Gabriel Ibels
Libert: La Scala
Published in ***Le café-concert,*** 1893
Lithograph printed in black
h. 34.5 x w. 24 cm.

A portrayal of Libert is included in Toulouse-Lautrec's illustrations for Gustave Geffroy's "Le plaisir à Paris" for *Le Figaro illustré,* 1893 (fig. 99C).

69.* Henri-Gabriel Ibels
Emilenne d'Alençon: Répétition générale aux Folies-Bergères
Published in ***Le café-concert,*** 1893
Lithograph printed in black
h. 31 x w. 22.7 cm.

A Toulouse-Lautrec lithograph of this same subject was produced in the December 3, 1893, issue of *L'Escarmouche.*

70.* Adolphe-Léon Willette
A son ami Marty, 1894
Lithograph printed in black
h. 29.2 x w. 21.5 cm.

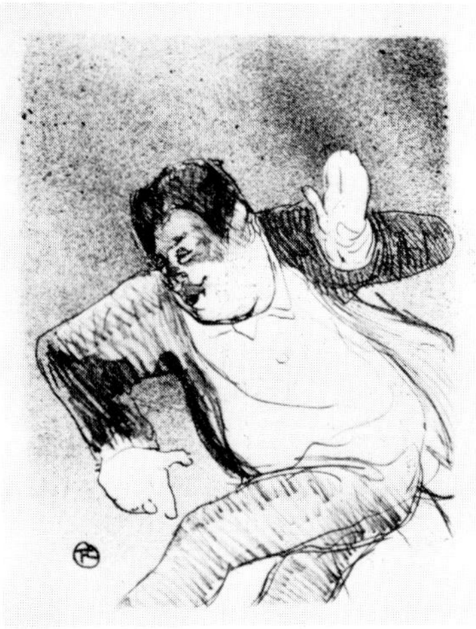

65

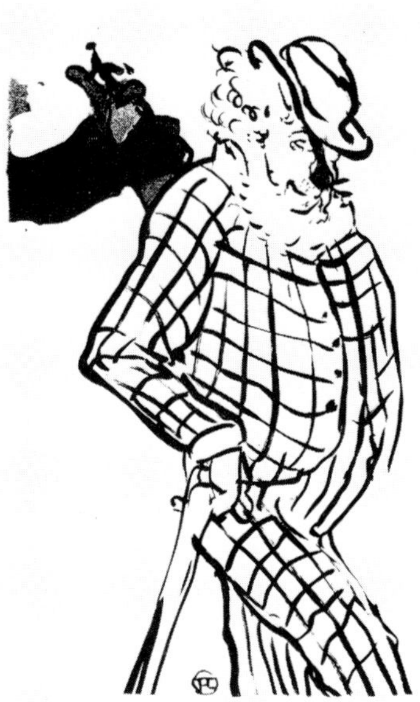

66

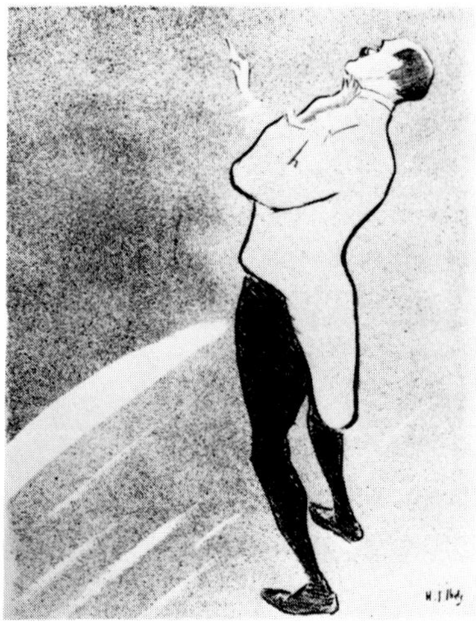

67

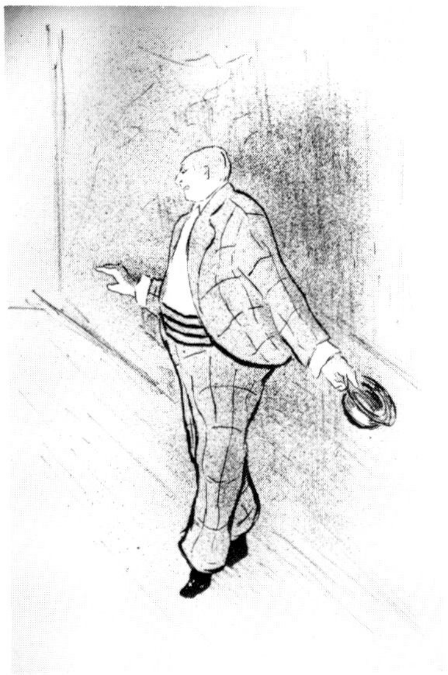

68

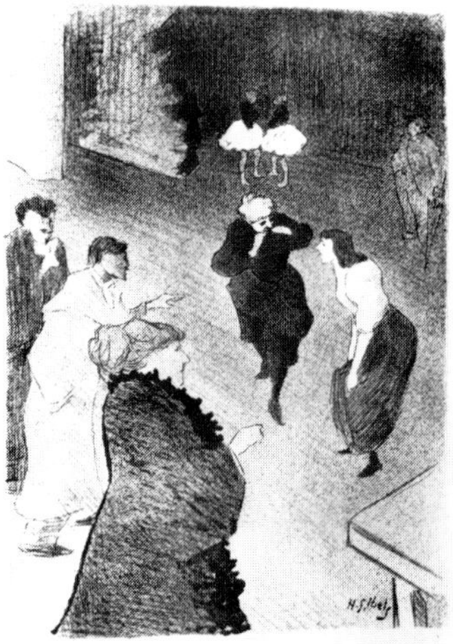

69

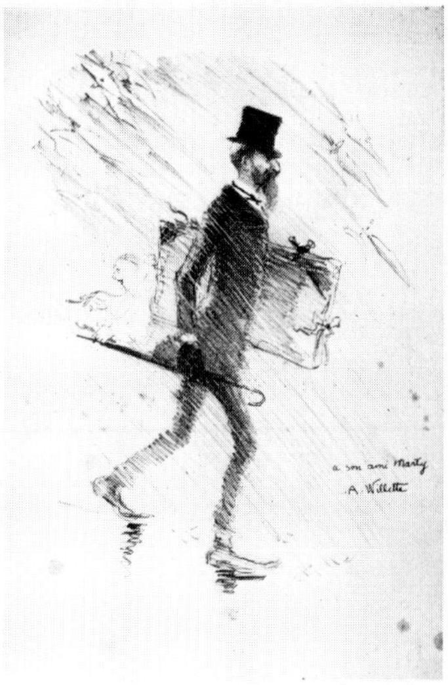

70

Adolphe-Léon Willette was born in Chalons-sur-Marne in 1857, the son of a military *aide-de-camp.* The family moved to Paris in 1864. Willette attended the École des Beaux-Arts in 1878-79 as a student of Cabanel. By 1886 he moved away from his earlier academic style and developed his own persona through *Le veuve de Pierrot,* with Pierrot and female nudes becoming the central themes of his work. He contributed generously to numerous periodicals and founded three himself: *Pierrot, Le pied de nez,* and *La vache enragée.*

In this lithograph of the publisher André Marty, Pierrot is shown escaping the portfolio he carries. Willette died in Paris in 1926.

71. Henri de Toulouse-Lautrec
Divan Japonais, c. 1905
Lithographic poster printed in four colors
h. 81 x w. 62 cm.

The *cabaret artistique* Divan Japonais was originally opened in 1888 by Jehan Serrazin. The originality of the café was its oriental decor. Until 1860 the site had been occupied by the Bal de l'Hermitage, an unpretentious tavern popular during the reign of Louis-Philippe. It was followed by the rowdy dance hall L'Elysée Buffet, which was finally closed in 1883. After partial demolition and renovation, the short-lived Taverne du Bagne opened for three months. Finally the structure was totally demolished and Divan Japonais was built.

Serrazin provided high quality entertainment, having an eye for discovering promising new talent. Here, Yvette Guilbert made her singing debut in 1891 with the song "Les vierges." In 1892 at the possible insistence of Jane Avril, Serrazin commissioned Toulouse-Lautrec to do the poster for Divan Japonais. Here, Toulouse-Lautrec produced his first lithographic portraits of both Jane Avril, seated prominently in the foreground, and Yvette Guilbert on stage. Although headless, she can be recognized by her unmistakable long, black kid-skin gloves. Jane Avril is accompanied by Edouard Dujardin, music critic, novelist, and founder of the *Revue Wagnerienne*. This poster was Toulouse-Lautrec's only professional link with this cabaret.

In 1892 Serrazin sold Divan Japonais to his former director Edouard Fournier. Fournier in turn sold the premises to Maxime Lisbonne of the Taverne du Bagne who renamed it Concert Lisbonne in 1893. Today, the space remains a cabaret, Madame Arthur, and features female impersonators.

72. Henri de Toulouse-Lautrec
Divan Japonais
Published by ***Les maîtres de l'affiche,*** 1896
Lithograph printed in four colors
h. 26.4 x w. 20 cm.

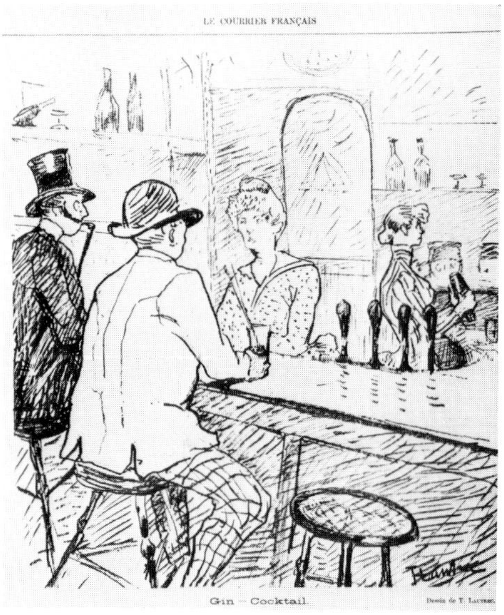

73

73.* Henri de Toulouse-Lautrec
Gin Cocktail
Published in ***Le courrier français,***
September 26, 1886
Photomechanical print in black
h. 22 x w. 20.5 cm.

Gin Cocktail is the first illustration by Toulouse-Lautrec to be reproduced in a periodical. *Le courrier français* was founded by Jules Roques in 1884 and specialized in cartoons and articles pertaining to Montmartre nightlife. Originally beginning weekly publication with its editorial office located in the back room of Le Rat Mort, a fashionable eating and drinking establishment frequented by lesbians on the Place Pigalle, the offices were later located in the Latin Quarter's rue Sequier.

Roques disliked Toulouse-Lautrec. He disapproved of his morals and found his talent unwholesome and his influence pernicious. Roques's feelings for Toulouse-Lautrec were interesting considering that *Le courrier français* defiantly published illegal nudes in modern settings (as opposed to legal nudes in allegorical or historical contexts). Numerous times each year, issues were seized by officials when cartoons or articles were deemed "an outrage to public morals." *Le courrier français* played the role of defender of freedom of the press and of artistic expression in general and was probably the foremost voice of the hedonistic *belle époque,* which it helped to create. Contributors regularly attacked the censorship of plays and songs in the theaters and music halls. In 1888 Roques came to the defense of street performers who were under attack for creating noise and uncleanliness. Toulouse-Lautrec submitted four additional illustrations to Roques in 1889, but they were not published by *Le courrier français.*

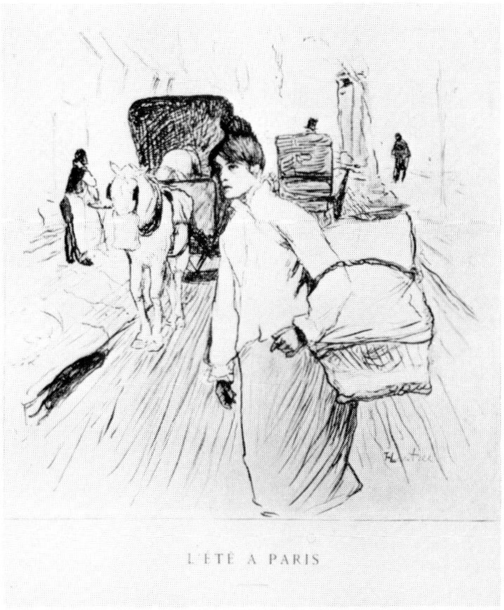

74

74.* Henri de Toulouse-Lautrec
L'Été à Paris: La blanchisseuse
Published in ***Paris illustré,*** July 7, 1888
Photomechanical print in black
h. 20.5 x w. 21.5 cm.

Paris illustré was published by the Galerie Boussod Valadon and edited by Maurice Joyant. Joyant was Toulouse-Lautrec's closest friend and primary biographer. In 1888 *Paris illustré* published these four illustrations that had previously been commissioned by Jules Roques in 1886 for *Le courrier français. Le cotier des omnibus* is on the reverse side of the double illustration (figs. 75, 75A). The four were used to illustrate the article "L'Été à Paris" by Émile Michelet.

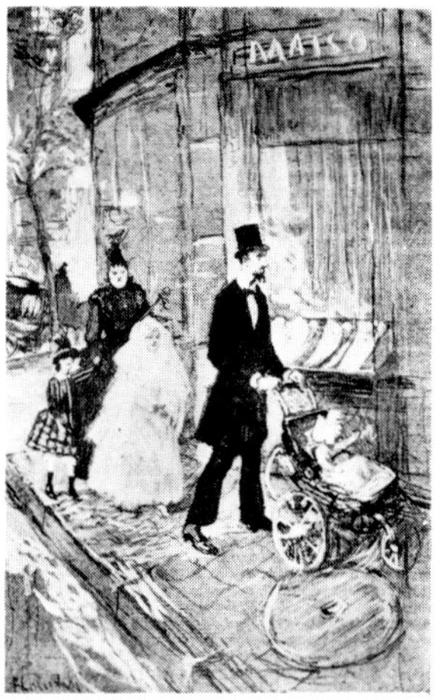

75

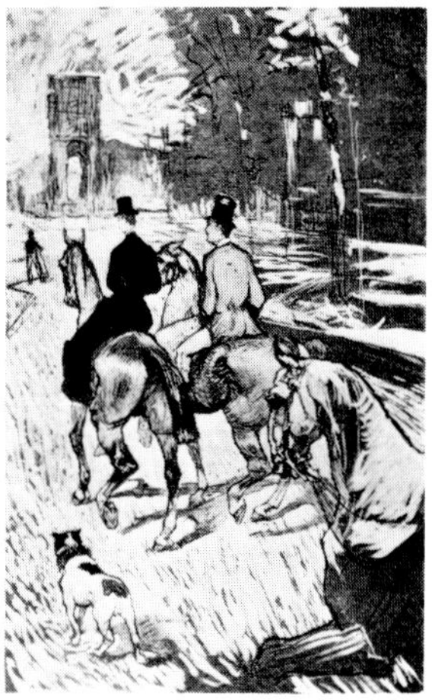

75A

75.* Henri de Toulouse-Lautrec
L'Été à Paris: Jour de première communion
L'Été à Paris: Cavaliers se rendant au bois
Published in ***Paris illustré,*** July 7, 1888
Photomechanical prints in black
(each) h. 17.3 x w. 11 cm.

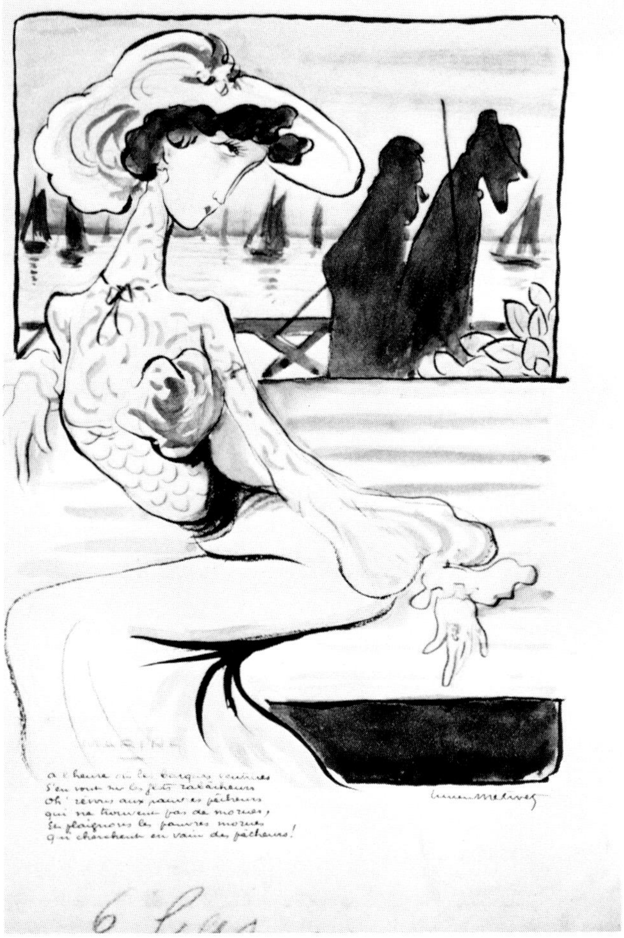

76.* Lucien Marie Françoise Métivet
Marine
Original design for ***Le Rire,*** September 17, 1904
Watercolor, ink, and gouache on paper
h. 32.6 x w. 23.7 cm.

77. Lucien Marie Françoise Métivet
Marine
Published in ***Le Rire,*** September 17, 1904
Color photomechanical print
h. 31. x w. 23.5 cm.

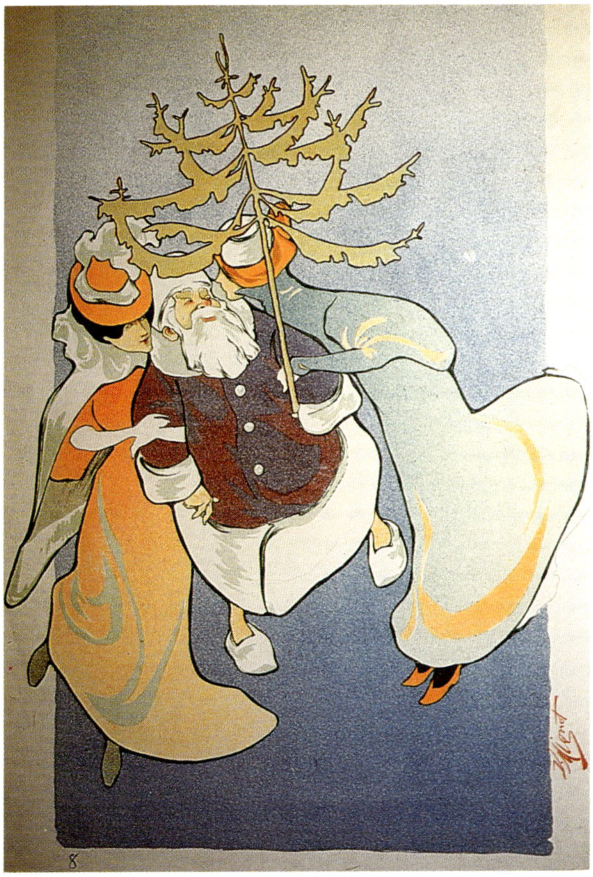

32

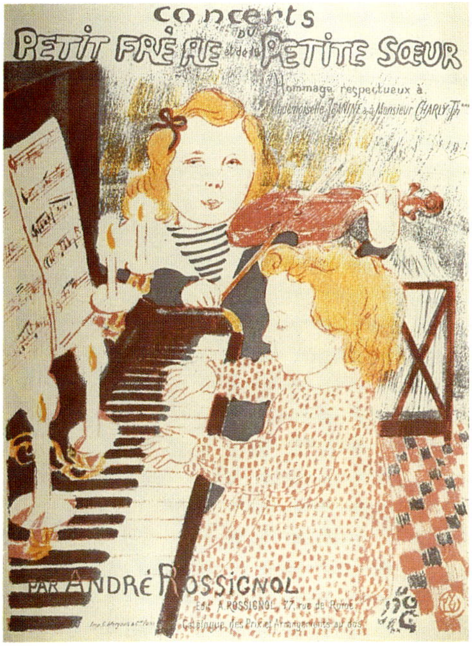
concerts
du
PETIT FRÈRE
et de la
PETITE SOEUR
Hommage respectueux à
Mademoiselle JEANINE et à Monsieur CHARLY
PAR ANDRÉ ROSSIGNOL
Ed. A. ROSSIGNOL, 57, rue de Rome

57

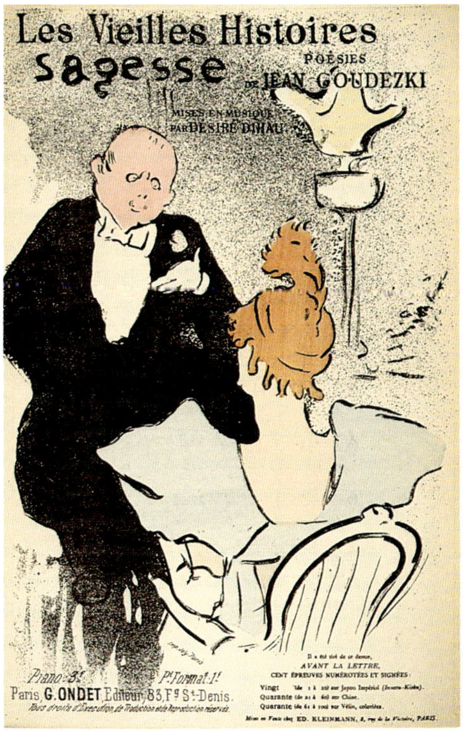
Les Vieilles Histoires
Sagesse
POÉSIES
DE JEAN GOUDEZKI
MISES EN MUSIQUE
PAR DÉSIRÉ DIHAU
Piano: 3f
Pt Format: 1f
Paris, G. ONDET Editeur, 83, Fg St-Denis.
Tous droits d'Exécution, de Traduction et de Reproduction réservés.
AVANT LA LETTRE,
CENT ÉPREUVES NUMÉROTÉES ET SIGNÉES:
Vingt
Quarante
Quarante
Mise en Vente chez ED. KLEINMANN, 8, rue de la Victoire, PARIS.

59

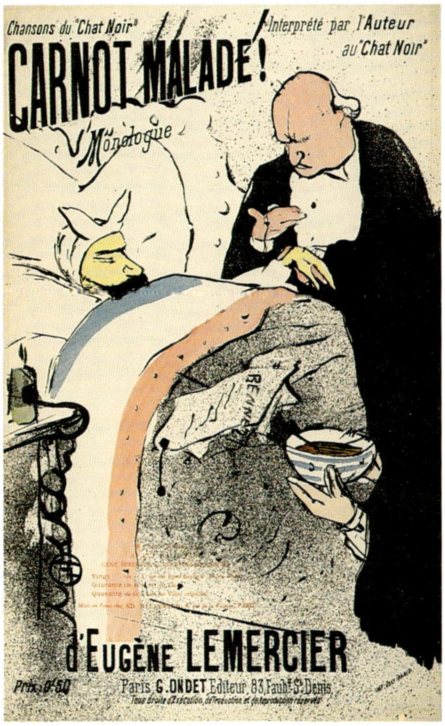
Chansons du "Chat Noir"
Interprété par l'Auteur
au "Chat Noir"
CARNOT MALADE!
Monologue
d'Eugène LEMERCIER
Prix: 0f50
Paris G. ONDET Editeur, 83, Faubg St Denis

60

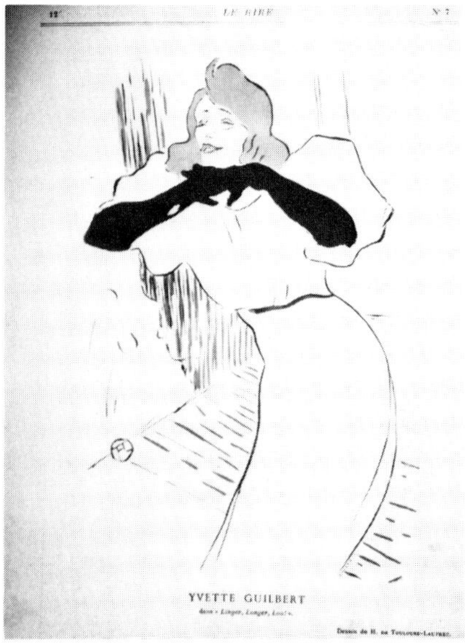

78

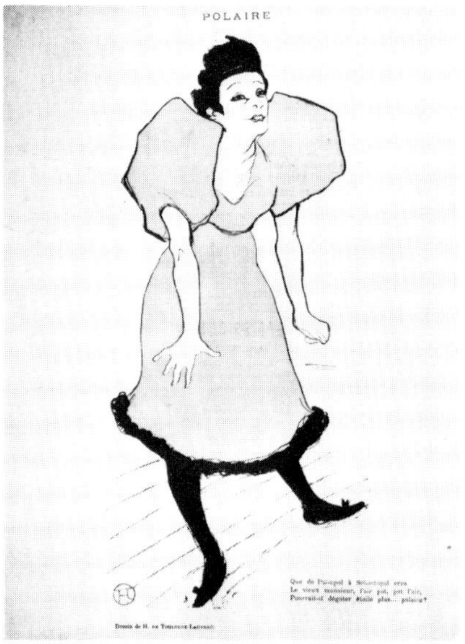

79

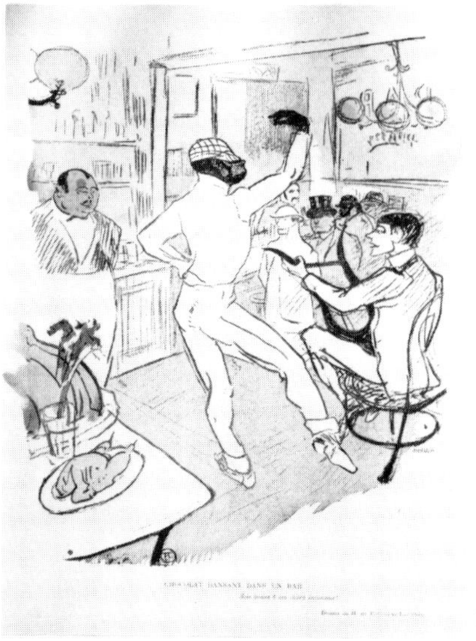

83

78.* Henri de Toulouse-Lautrec
Yvette Guilbert in "Linger, Longer, Loo!"
Published in ***Le Rire,*** November 10, 1894
Photomechanical print in four colors
h. 31 x w. 23.5 cm.

Le Rire, the weekly satirical and humorous journal, was founded November 10, 1894, by art critic and writer Arsène Alexandre and Félix Juven. It allowed many of *Le courrier français's* artists who worked only in black and white to take advantage of the four-color (red, yellow, blue, and black) relief-plate process.

Yvette Guilbert was the first illustration that Toulouse-Lautrec contributed to *Le Rire;* there were to be 18 in all. Born Emma-Louise-Esther Guilbert on January 20, 1868, in Paris, Yvette, as she was known, began her career at age 15. Following the failure of her debut in 1889 at L'Eldorado, she realized that her voice was ideally suited to the *café-concert.* After two successful seasons at the Eden Concert, where she refined her appearance and repertoire, she was featured regularly at the Moulin Rouge and the Divan Japonais and later at the Concert Parisian, La Scala, Les Ambassadeurs, and L'Horloge.

Toulouse-Lautrec's first encounter with Yvette Guilbert occurred in July 1894 when he offered to design a poster for her. She rejected the design in favor of one by Steinlen and protested to Toulouse-Lautrec by letter, "But for the love of heaven, don't make me so atrociously ugly." However, it was inevitable that Yvette sat in person for this *Le Rire* drawing. In the early fall of 1894, Toulouse-Lautrec produced a 16-lithograph *Album d'Yvette Guilbert* with text by Gustave Geffroy, published by André Marty. Once again, she was appalled by his caricatures but was appeased when several articles praising the album appeared in various journals. After that, Guilbert accepted Toulouse-Lautrec's interpretations without protest.

79.* Henri de Toulouse-Lautrec
Polaire
Published in ***Le Rire,*** February 23, 1895
Photomechanical print in three colors
h. 31 x w. 23.5 cm.

This striking portrait of the singer Polaire was probably drawn around March 1894 during her prestigious and successful engagement at Les Ambassadeurs. Born Emilie Zouze-Bouchard in Algeria in 1879, Polaire was scarcely more than a child when she began earning her livelihood as a singer in the lesser Parisian *cafés -concerts.* She made her debut at La Cigalle. Her dramatic talent and curious gypsy vitality quickly made her a popular idol, not only as a singer but as a leading comedic actress. Polaire appeared with Jane Avril in the original production of *Claudine à Paris* at the Bouffes-Parisian.

80. Henri de Toulouse-Lautrec
Snobisme
Cover for ***Le Rire,*** April 24, 1897
Photomechanical print in four colors
h. 31 x w. 23.5 cm.

81. Henri de Toulouse-Lautrec
Alors vous êtes sage?
Cover for ***Le Rire,*** January 9, 1897
Photomechanical print in four colors
h. 31 x w. 23.5 cm.

82. Henri de Toulouse-Lautrec
Aux Folies-Bergères: Brothers Marco
Published in ***Le Rire,*** December 22, 1895
Photomechanical print in three colors
h. 31 x w. 23.5 cm.

83.* Henri de Toulouse-Lautrec
Chocolat dansant dans un bar
Published in ***Le Rire,*** March 28, 1896
Photomechanical print in five colors
h. 31 x w. 23.5 cm.

Chocolat, the black clown, acrobat, and mime, was half the team of Footit & Chocolat that performed at the Nouveau Cirque in Paris. Chocolat is seen here dancing in the Irish and American Bar in the Place Madeleine. Looking on are the bartender, Ralph, and in the rear Tom, the top-hatted coachman of one of the de Rothschild barons. All three are frequently pictured in works by Toulouse-Lautrec.

84.* Torrès
El gato negro, c. 1895
Lithographic poster printed in five colors
h. 81.7 x w. 50.5 cm.

This poster was for the Spanish newspaper *El gato negro* that brought news of the homeland to the growing Spanish community in Paris. These Spanish expatriates included Picasso among others.

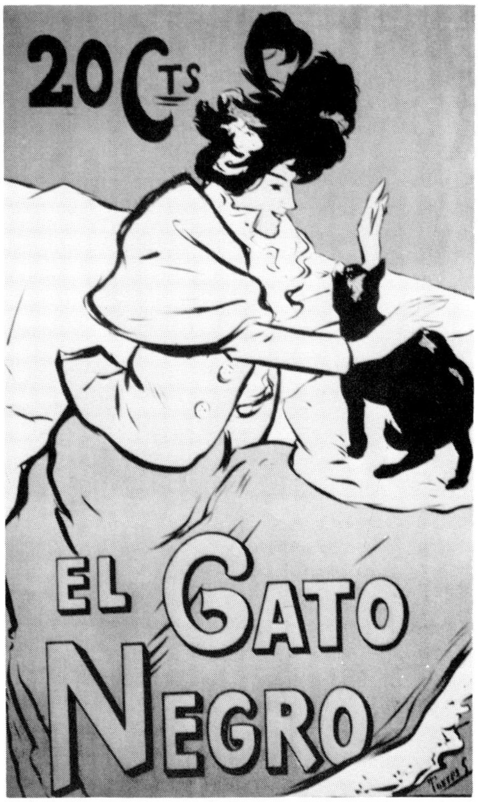

84

85.* Théophile-Alexandre Steinlen
Nathalie Madoré, 1895
Lithographic book cover printed in three colors
h. 20 x w. 27 cm.

This book cover was for the French edition of Abel Hermant's novel *Nathalie Madoré* published in Paris and Leipzig in 1895.

Théophile-Alexandre Steinlen was born in Lausanne, Switzerland, in 1859. After studying at the University of Lausanne, Steinlen served an apprenticeship in Mulhouse. He moved to Paris in 1881. By 1883 he was associated with Rodolphe Salis and the Chat Noir. By 1885 Steinlen, under the pseudonym Jean Caillou, regularly began making illustrations for *Le Mirliton.* He also designed posters and literally thousands of magazine illustrations for numerous periodicals and produced many prints, book jackets, and song sheet illustrations. As in the case of Toulouse-Lautrec, Steinlen also made his first color illustrations for *Le Mirliton,* and it was he who developed the economical system of stencil coloring.

86.* Théophile-Alexandre Steinlen
Asche, 1895
Lithographic book cover printed in five colors
h. 20 x w. 27 cm.

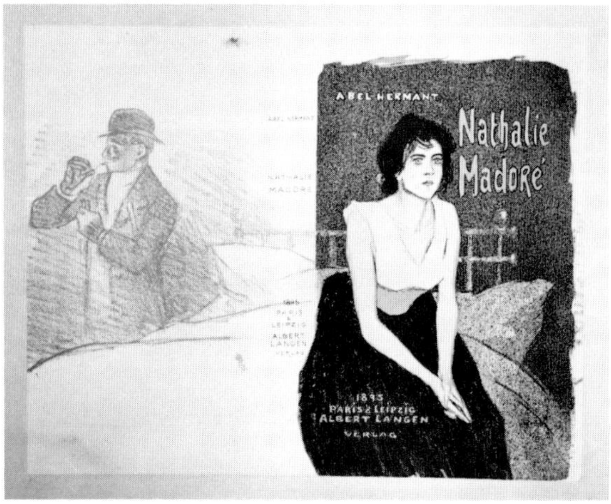

85

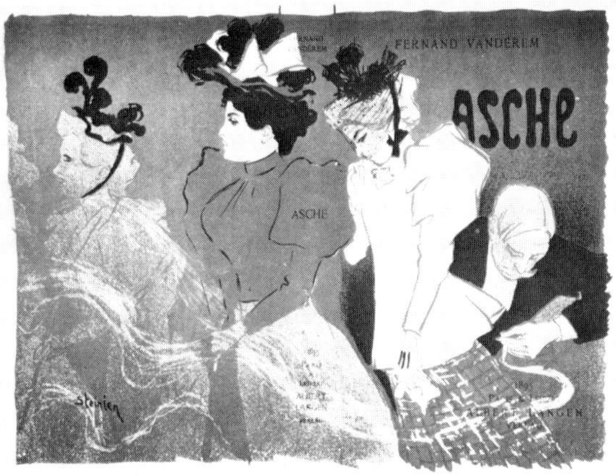

86

87. Jules Chéret
Graine d'horizontales, c. 1890
Lithographic book cover printed in three colors
h. 19.5 x w. 29 cm.

88. Paul Balluriau
Le dernier bateau, 1900
Lithographic book cover printed in three colors
h. 18.7 x w. 27 cm.

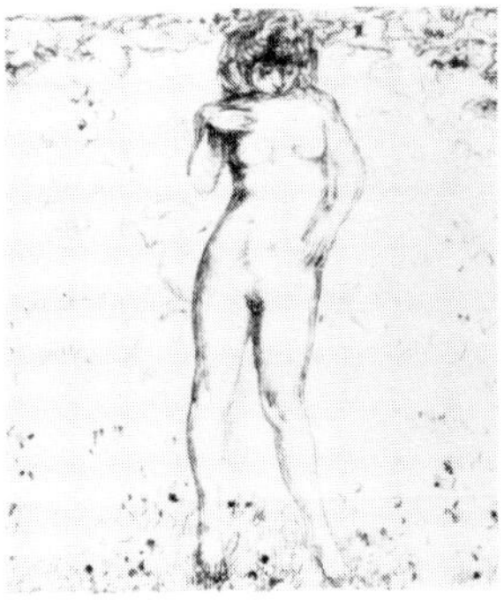

89

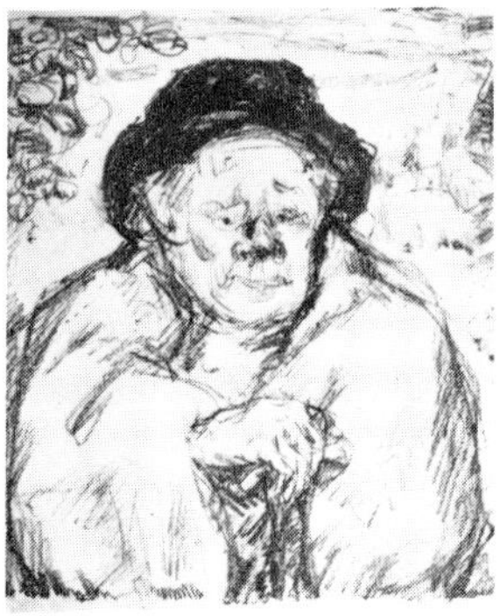

90

89.* Pierre Bonnard
Chloé Bathing
Illustration for ***Daphnis and Chloé,*** 1902
Lithographic proof printed in black
h. 15.2 x w. 14 cm.

This and the following lithographic proof (fig. 90) were made for *Daphnis and Chloé,* a romantic fourth- or fifth-century pastoral Greek poem attributed to Longus. *Daphnis and Chloé* was the second illustrated book commissioned from Bonnard by the publisher Ambroise Vollard. It was more classically inspired and proved to be considerably more popular than the earlier *Parallelement.* Printed in 1902 at the Imprimerie Nationale by Auguste Clot and published by Vollard in an edition of 250, it contained 156 standard, squarish-format lithographs and six variations.

Daphnis and Chloé had originally been translated from Greek into French in 1559 by Jacques Amyot for François I and was revised in 1810 by Paul-Louis Courier. It relates the adventures of a young goatherd and a shepherdess on the island of Lesbos. Abandoned as babies and growing up in love, the protagonists are separated, but rejoined in marriage in the end to live happily ever after united with each other and reunited with their no-less-than-noble parents.

90.* Pierre Bonnard
Personnage masculin en buste
Variant design for ***Daphnis and Chloé,*** 1902
Lithograph printed in black
h. 15.5 x w. 14 cm.

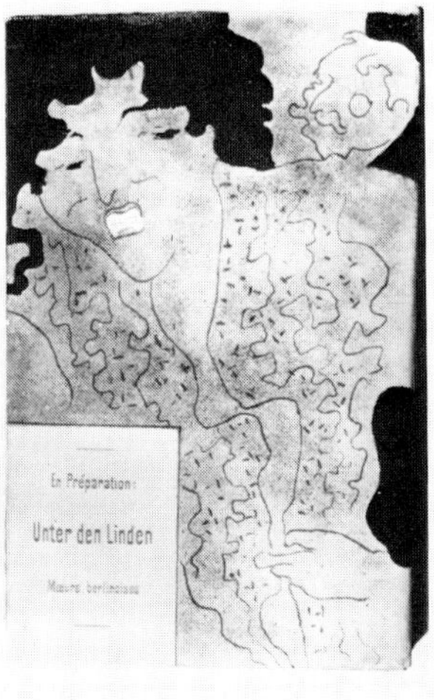

91A

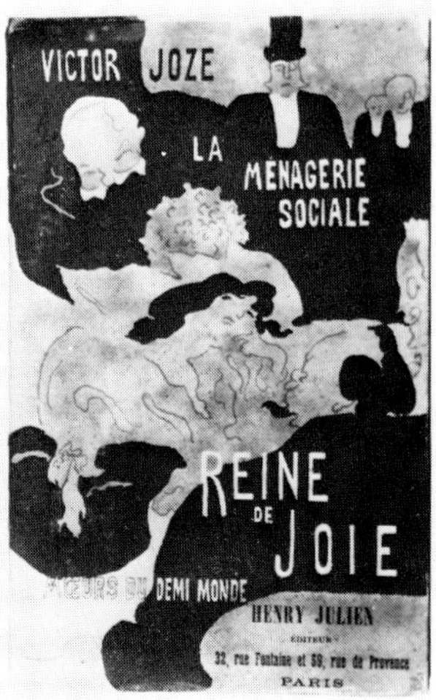

91

91.* Pierre Bonnard
Reine de joie, 1892
Lithographic book cover printed in four colors
h. 26 x w. 19 cm.

Reine de joie is a little-known book by Victor Joze (pen name for the Polish novelist Victor Dobrski) published in 1892 by Henry Jullien.

Bonnard was commissioned to design the book cover while the frontispiece depicts Toulouse-Lautrec's poster advertising the book (no. 92). The poster/frontispiece shows two characters from the book, Hélène Roland, the heroine, kissing the fat Olizac before he leaves for Paris. The book caused a scandal in the Parisian banking world, because the Baron de Rothschild thought he recognized himself in the hero, Baron de Rosenfeld, and sought to stop the sale of this anti-Semitic work. The newspaper that reported the scandal and prompted the writing of the book bought up the remaining copies and posters and sold them, probably with anti-Semitic motives. The posters already on the streets were torn from the walls by interested parties and confiscated by the police.

92. Henri de Toulouse-Lautrec
Reine de joie, 1892
Lithographic frontispiece printed in four colors
h. 12.5 x w. 8.7 cm.

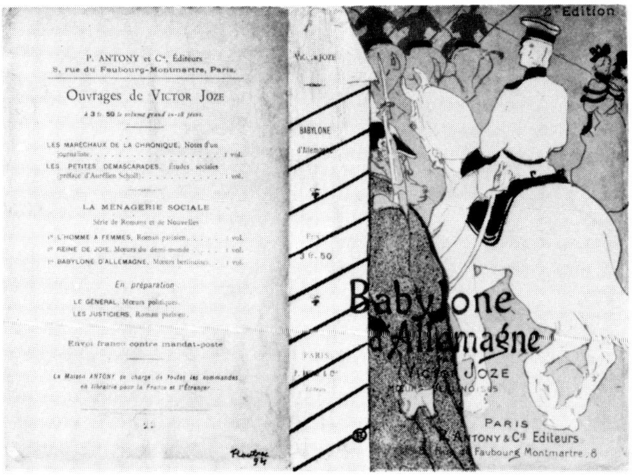

93

93.* Henri de Toulouse-Lautrec
Babylone d'Allemagne, 1894
Lithographic book cover printed in three colors
(front cover) h. 18.8 x w. 11.5 cm.

Toulouse-Lautrec illustrated this book cover as well as the poster advertising *Babylone d'Allemagne* by Victor Joze. Like *Reine de joie,* this novel too created a stir. The arrogance of the mounted Prussian officer in the illustration lampooned the German military, offending the German ambassador and nearly setting off an international incident.

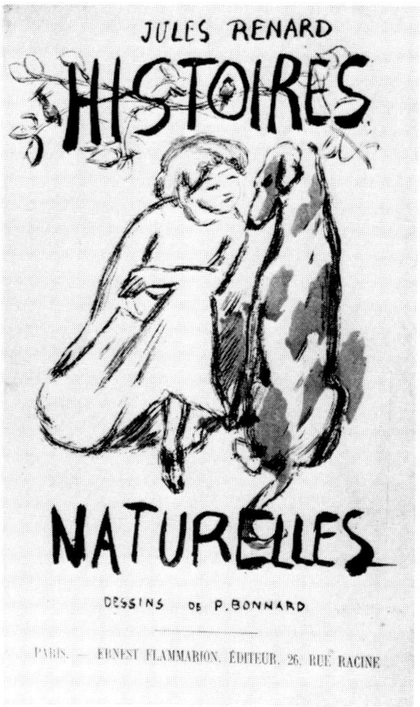

94

94.* Pierre Bonnard
Histoires naturelles
Illustrated book for Jules Renard, 1904
Photomechanical print with two stenciled colors
h. 18 x w. 11 cm.

Histoires naturelles ("Natural History") by Jules Renard has a two-color stenciled cover and is illustrated by 67 process prints from original Japanese-inspired ink drawings by Bonnard. It was published by Ernest Flammarion and printed by Hammerle and Company, Paris; reprints in 1922 and 1945 have varying layouts and covers.

Toulouse-Lautrec had originally illustrated the book in 1899 with 23 transfer lithographs, but Renard did not care for his illustrations. After the artist's death in 1901, he commissioned Bonnard to illustrate this new version.

The back cover of the book advertises another book by Renard, *Poil de Carrotte,* with illustrations by Félix Vallotton.

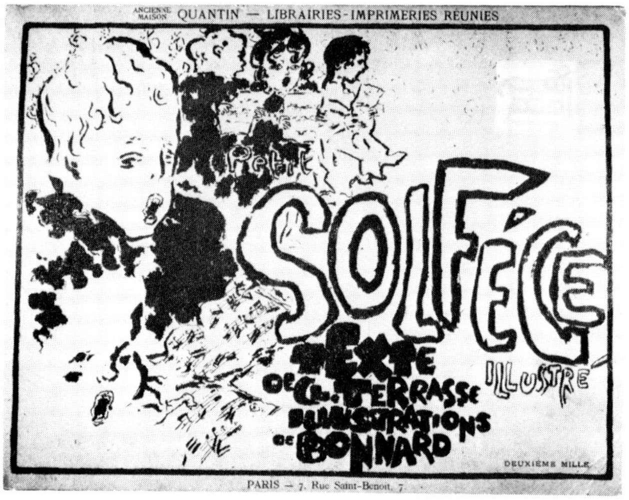

95

95.* Pierre Bonnard
Petit solfège illustré
Illustrated music book for Claude Terrasse, 1893
Lithographic book cover printed in blue
h. 21.2 x w. 28.3 cm.

Collaboration began early in 1891 on *Petit solfège illustré,* the music theory primer for children written by Terrasse and illustrated by Bonnard. The book contains 32 lithographic illustrations including the front and back covers. It was published by Libraries-Imprimeries Reuniés, Ancienne Maison Quantin of Paris in 1893 and printed by F. Allier Père et Fils of Grenoble in an edition of 2000.

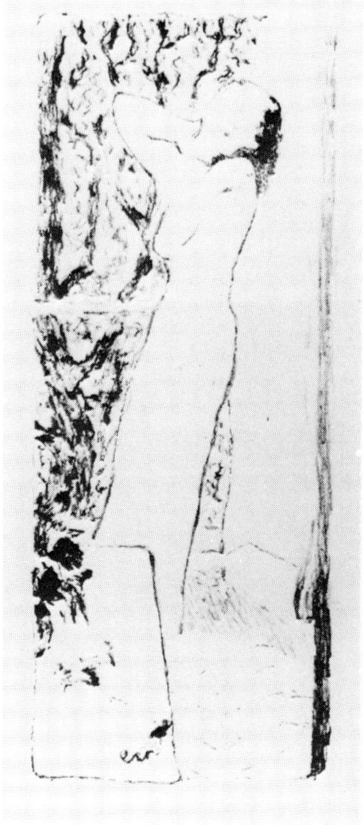

96

96.* Edouard Vuillard
Frontispiece for ***Nouvelles passionnées,*** 1893
Lithograph printed in green
h. 18.9 x w. 7.5 cm.

This lithograph for Maurice Beaubourg's novel *Nouvelles passionnées* was published by *La revue blanche* in 1893.

97. Jules-Alexandre Grün
Chansons...Rosses
Illustrated book of songs for Henri Fursy, 1905
Photomechanical print in two colors
h. 17 x w. 10.3 cm.

98.** Fernand Toussaint(?)
Grands magasins de nouveautés
Promotional fan, c. 1895
Lithograph printed in five colors
h. 18.5 x w. 18 cm.

Fernand Toussaint (1873-1956), a Belgian artist, may have designed this unsigned fan. The stippling and the coloration seen here are characteristic of his style and can be seen in his signed works.

99.* Henri de Toulouse-Lautrec
Le plaisir à Paris: Les restaurants et les cafés-concerts des Champs-Elysées
Two double-sided sheets published in ***Le Figaro illustré,*** 1893
Color photomechanical prints
(each) h. 42 x w. 32 cm.

Le Figaro illustré was a monthly periodical published by the gallery and art firm of Boussod, Valadon et Cie. It featured full-color photomechanical illustrations to accompany the text and was printed on high quality, coated papers (nos. 100-103; fig. 100B).

100.* Henri de Toulouse-Lautrec
La plaisir à Paris: Les bals et le carnaval
Two double-sided sheets published in ***Le Figaro illustré,*** 1894
Color photomechanical prints
(each) h. 42 x w. 32 cm.

101. Henri de Toulouse-Lautrec
La belle et la bête
Double-sided sheet published in ***Le Figaro illustré,*** 1895
Color photomechanical print
h. 42 x w. 32 cm.

102. Henri de Toulouse-Lautrec
Le bon jockey
Double-sided sheet published in ***Le Figaro illustré,*** 1895
Color photomechanical print
h. 42 x w. 32 cm.

103. Henri de Toulouse-Lautrec
Les deux soeurs légendaires
Double-sided sheet published in ***Le Figaro illustré,*** 1896
Color photomechanical print
h. 42 x w. 32 cm.

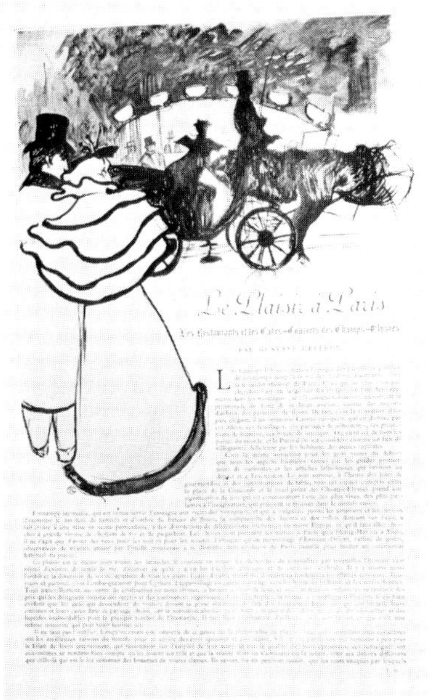

99

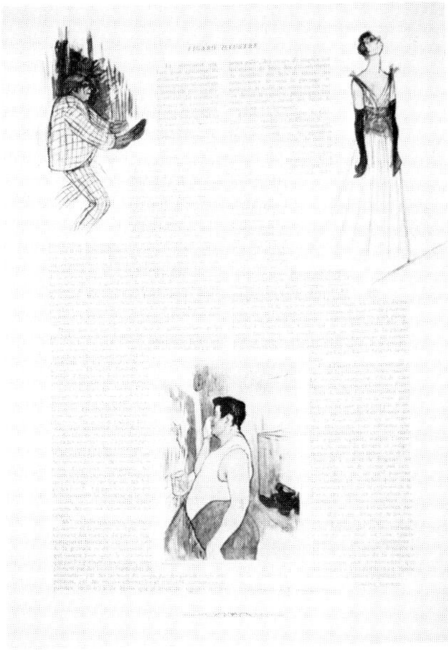

99C

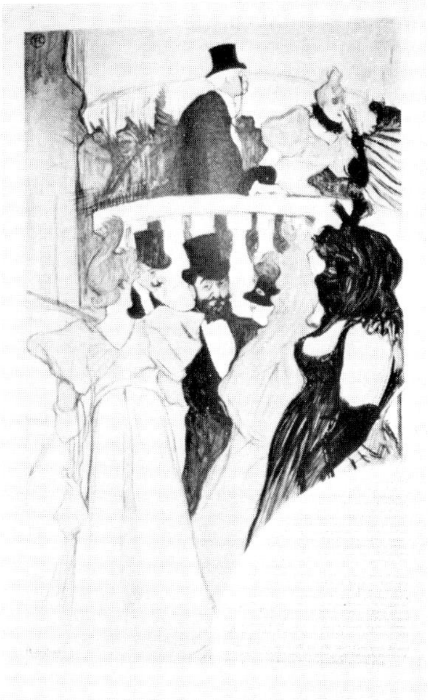

100B

Bibliography

Artists of La Revue Blanche. Rochester, N.Y.: Memorial Art Gallery of the University of Rochester, 1984.

Bouvet, Francis. *Bonnard: The Complete Graphic Work*. New York, 1981.

Boyer, Patricia Eckert, and Elizabeth Prelinger. *The Nabis and the Parisian Avant-Garde*. New Brunswick, N.J., 1988.

Boyle-Turner, Caroline. *Paul Sérusier*. Ann Arbor, Mich., 1983.

____. *The Prints of the Pont-Aven School: Gauguin and his Circle in Brittany*. Foreword by Douglas Druick. New York, 1986.

Broido, Lucy. *The Posters of Jules Chéret*. New York, 1980.

Carey, Frances, and Anthony Griffiths. *From Manet to Toulouse-Lautrec: French Lithographs 1860-1900*. London: British Museum, 1978.

Castleman, Riva, and Wolfgang Wittrock, eds. *Henri de Toulouse-Lautrec: Images of the 1890s*. New York: The Museum of Modern Art, 1985.

Cate, Phillip D., and Patricia E. Boyer. *The Circle of Toulouse-Lautrec: An Exhibition of the Work of the Artist and his Close Associates*. New Brunswick, N.J.: Rutgers University Art Gallery, 1980.

Cate, Phillip Dennis, and Sinclair Hamilton Hitchings. *The Color Revolution: Color Lithography in France 1890-1900*. New Brunswick, N.J.: Rutgers University Art Gallery, 1978.

David, Jean-Luc. *Modern Art 1884-1914*. New York, 1979.

Druick, Douglas, and Peter Zegers. *La Pierre Parle: Lithography in France 1848-1900* (exhibition text panels and labels). Ottawa: National Gallery of Canada, 1981.

Ives, Colta Feller. *The Great Wave*. New York: The Metropolitan Museum of Art, 1974.

Perruchot, Henri. *Toulouse-Lautrec*. Translated by Humphrey Ware. New York, 1962.

Rewald, John. *Pierre Bonnard*. New York, 1948.

Roger-Marx, Claude. *L'Oeuvre gravé de Vuillard*. Monte Carlo, 1948.

Russell, John. *Edouard Vuillard 1868-1940*. Toronto: Art Gallery of Ontario, 1971.

Terrasse, Antoine. *Pierre Bonnard*. Paris, 1967.

____. *Pierre Bonnard: Illustrator*. London, 1989.

Thomson, Belinda. *Vuillard*. Oxford, 1988.

Weber, Eugen. *France, Fin de Siècle*. Cambridge, Mass., 1986.

Wittrock, Wolfgang. *Toulouse-Lautrec: The Complete Prints*. 2 vols. London, 1985.

Zeldin, Theodore. *France 1848-1945: Intellect and Pride*. 1st ed., 1977; reprint, Oxford, 1980.